Empath Guide:

This Books Includes:

Empath:

The Most Effective Empath Healing and Empath Survival Guide in Today's World for Highly Sensitive People to Protect Yourself and Enjoy Life. Empath Rising!

Enneagram:

The Only Book You Will Ever Need to Build Strength for Your Life. Discover The 9 Personalities Types. Evolve Your Personality and Become Self Aware!

Empath:
The Most Effective Empath Healing and Empath Survival Guide in Today's World for Highly Sensitive People to Protect Yourself and Enjoy Life. Empath Rising!

Table of Contents

Introduction……………………………………………………………5

Chapter One: What Does It Mean to Be an Empath?…………7

Chapter Two: Understanding an Empath………………………14

Chapter Three: How to Have Healthy Relationships…………22

Chapter Four: How to Be a Parent as an Empath……………33

Chapter Five: How to Thrive in the World of Work as an Empath…………………………………………………………………36

Chapter Six: Why Some Empaths Turn to Addiction…………45

Chapter Seven: How to Protect Yourself as an Empath……48

Chapter Eight: The Benefits of Meditation……………………57

Chapter Nine: How Empaths Have Helped the World………66

Conclusion……………………………………………………………69

© Copyright 2018 by Judith Guise - All rights reserved.

The follow eBook is reproduced below with the goal of providing information that is as accurate and reliable as possible. Regardless, purchasing this eBook can be seen as consent to the fact that both the publisher and the author of this book are in no way experts on the topics discussed within and that any recommendations or suggestions that are made herein are for entertainment purposes only. Professionals should be consulted as needed prior to undertaking any of the action endorsed herein.

This declaration is deemed fair and valid by both the American Bar Association and the Committee of Publishers Association and is legally binding throughout the United States.

Furthermore, the transmission, duplication or reproduction of any of the following work including specific information will be considered an illegal act irrespective of if it is done electronically or in print. This extends to creating a secondary or tertiary copy of the work or a recorded copy and is only allowed with express written consent from the Publisher. All additional right reserved.

The information in the following pages is broadly considered to be a truthful and accurate account of facts and as such any inattention, use or misuse of the information in question by the reader will render any resulting actions solely under their purview. There are no scenarios in which the publisher or the original author of this work can be in any fashion deemed liable for any hardship or damages that may befall them after undertaking information described herein.

Additionally, the information in the following pages is intended only for informational purposes and should thus be thought of as universal. As befitting its nature, it is presented without assurance regarding its prolonged validity or interim quality. Trademarks that are mentioned are done without written consent and can in no way be considered an endorsement from the trademark holder.

Introduction

In a high-stimulus world, many people struggle with the onslaught of input in various forms. Our senses are bombarded, and if limits are not set, this bombardment and sensory overload can be continuous. Research has shown that our autonomous nervous systems are becoming extra sensitive because of this overload. This leads to all kinds of ailments like hormone imbalances and compromised immune systems. Empaths have to deal with this in an exponentially greater way. They are wired to feel things so much more deeply and passionately. Empaths not only feel all these emotions but absorb and take on the energies of people that they are surrounded with. The more people, the more chaos, the more they absorb the turmoil and negativity.

Empaths rely on their feelings and intuition as the filter through which they interact with the world. They are giving, compassionate, excellent friends, but one of the most attractive qualities of empaths is their ability to completely understand you and to truly listen. This can leave empaths open and vulnerable to abuse by others, emotional exhaustion and the need for isolation. This often leaves them misunderstood by others, relegating them to a world of seclusion or addiction.
This book explores what it is to be an empath. It explores the ideas around what, and more importantly, why they are experiencing what they do. Empaths and people surrounded by empaths can better understand their behaviors and responses in situations and can be better equipped to help them if necessary or be a support structure for them. Many empaths can result in depressions, social anxiety, panic attacks or a range of addictions if they do not understand what is happening to them and how to protect themselves. This book will teach you that empaths do not need to feel overwhelmed all the time. By recognition, understanding, and acceptance, one can navigate the world successfully. It is also meant to inspire empaths to embrace their purpose in life by looking at how some famous

empaths changed the world. This book provides techniques and tools to live a fuller, happier life as an empath.

This book is to validate and affirm empaths who may be feeling confused and overwhelmed. Whether you are, or someone you know is an empath, this will help you gain a better understanding and appreciation of what it means to be an empath in the modern world. This is extremely important as it can change our world.

Chapter One: What Does It Mean to Be an Empath?

Who is an empath? Have you found that you become extremely emotional around pain, cruelty, and loss, to the point where you will not watch certain movies, the news, or you find yourself staying away from social media? Do you find that this emotion can stay with you for days and that it can be difficult to shake off? Perhaps you were always told that you were too sensitive as a child. Sometimes you feel misunderstood by people thinking you are avoiding relevant and topical issues, and you should rather be pro-active in trying to solve them. People do not understand that the emotion you feel can be crippling. If any of this feels familiar to you, you may well be an empath.

Living in a world filled with injustice, pain, and suffering can be very daunting for an empath. As you might have guessed, the word empath comes from 'empathy'. The dictionary defines empathy as the ability to relate, understand, and share the feelings of someone else. Empaths do this, but it is on an exponentially deeper level. Empaths, therefore absorb the energies of the world, this can be negative ones associated with stress and pain or positive ones associated with joy and love. Experiencing these emotions to such an extreme level can make one feel slightly lost and misunderstood by others. You can feel like you just don't belong. However, being an empath can be one of the greatest skills you can have if you learn how to live with it.

Empaths are people who are extremely susceptible to the emotions of others. This ability to relate so personally to others makes empaths one of the best nurturers, listeners, and givers that you will find. Empaths compassion for people can leave them feeling exhausted, but the good news is that they can develop strategies to create boundaries and protect their feelings.

Scientific Theories

For those skeptics who think empaths belong to the category of fairies and folktales, there are five interesting scientific arguments for empaths and empathy.

Electromagnetic Fields
The heart and brain both create electromagnetic fields which transmit information about people's feelings and thoughts. Empaths are incredibly sensitive to these fields. These fields can be documented and provide scientific evidence of what empaths engage with.

Mirror Neuron System
It has been discovered that there are cells in the brain that mirror people's emotions. When your child is hurt at school, you feel hurt too. When your spouse gets an increase, you feel their joy as well. Empaths are thought to have hyper-sensitive mirror neurons compared to other people and therefore can relate to and feel deep compassion for others—even strangers. Conversely, "*empathy deficient disorders*" like sociopaths, psychopaths, narcissists, and even people with autism have desensitized mirror neurons and do not feel empathy toward others. Experiments have been done and measured through fMRI, which are basically scans of the brain activity. These scans show how closely scans of empaths and candidates match each other.

Emotional Contagion
Have you ever wondered why when one baby starts to cry, it sets off other babies around it? Or when you yawn you make people around you yawn? It is more common than you think for people to take on other people's emotions. This phenomenon is called emotional contagion. Research has even shown that this ability to synchronize feelings is important for relationships. Empaths experience this at a deeper level than most people.

Synesthesia
Synesthesia is when a person experiences more than one sense simultaneously. For example, a person could see colors when they listen to music. Isaac Newton is a well-known synesthetic. "*Mirror-touch synesthesia*" is a neurological condition where some rare individuals can actually experience similar sensations or emotions of others as if it were their own. For example, these people could feel an abdominal pain that they observe in another. Many empaths will relate to the "*Mirror-touch synesthesia*" condition.

Dopamine
Dopamine is a neurotransmitter that is linked with the pleasure response. There are many studies that have shown that dopamine affects the empathic perceptions and responses in people. People with a high sensitivity to dopamine need less dopamine to experience joy. They can take pleasure from simple activities like reading and walking in nature rather than high stimulation from parties etc. People with a low sensitivity to dopamine need to have to do a lot more to experience joy. Therefore it is understandable why empaths will readily feel the joy of others.

Empaths and Highly Sensitive People
Empaths are often confused with highly sensitive people. Highly sensitive people do not need much stimulation. They may experience sensitivity to the senses or avoid people and large crowds. They have things in common with empaths like alone time, helping others and a passion for nature. But empaths take these experiences to a higher level. They can sense and absorb the energy of others, sometimes to the extent that they can't distinguish it from their own emotions. Highly sensitive people and empaths are not mutually exclusive; there are many people who are both.

Characteristics of an Empath

If you have been able to identify with many of the traits already discussed, you may well be an empath or know of one. Here are a few more characteristics that may help you recognize the traits.

Empaths are Great Listeners
Because they can identify with what you are saying. They make amazing friends because they can relate to what you are feeling and will do whatever they can to help.

They are Nurturers and Caregivers
Whether good or bad, negative or positive, empaths will absorb these energies. If they take on more negative energies, they will feel exhausted; if they are surrounded by positive energies, they will thrive.

Empaths Do Not Cope Well in Crowds
They prefer to either be alone or have smaller social groups. This is a natural consequence of absorbing the energies around them. In crowds, this energy absorption is increased tenfold. The avoidance of crowds and large groups of people make empaths introverted people.

Empaths use their intuition
They use intuition to engage with the world, and therefore, have a highly developed sense of intuition. They need to take time to stop and recognize what they are feeling before it has any negative implications for them.

Alone Time Is Super Important for Empaths
It is the time they use to recharge and re-energize. This need for alone time often makes empaths shy away from intimate relationships. There may be an underlying fear that they absorb too much of the other person and lose themselves. There are some people that drain your energy or peace of mind. An empath is particularly vulnerable to these energy zappers, as

they are drawn from the emotional sensitivity of empaths and can eventually affect them negatively.

Everything Natural Replenishes, Revives and Restores an Empath

They take refuge in nature and seek out time in the wilderness. Empaths have highly sensitized senses and cannot cope with excessive noise, talking and smells. Empaths love to help people, but this leads to them taking on those energies to their own detriment.

Remember, being able to recognize if you are or anyone you know is an empath, is the first step. These established steps and guidelines can be followed to protect yourself and create balance.

The Making of an Empath

So what makes people become empaths? Is it nature? Or nurture? There are a number of reasons why people develop or intensify their sensitivities.

Nature

Many mothers will notice that their newborns are more sensitive to touch, smell, movement, sound, light, and temperature when they are born. This would suggest an inherent inclination towards being an empath. Sometimes empaths pass on these characteristics genetically to their offspring.

Nurture

The trauma suffered as a child may lead to increased sensitivity levels as an adult. These children may feel a greater sense of not being valued or heard as the trauma wears down their defenses. They may feel increasingly helpless as they take on negative emotions of those around them. Conversely, a supportive environment can see an empath child thrive into a healthy and powerful adult.

Whichever the cause, the symptoms are the same: crowds, bright lights, noise, an angry person—can all lead to a sensory overload for an empath. The important point to remember is that there is a way forward, and we address all the things you can do as an empath, no matter what your background—to understand, heal, and protect yourself.

Empaths, unlike other people, need to learn to defend themselves against stress, they are different. A noxious stimulus, such as an angry person, crowds, noise, or bright lights can agitate us since our threshold for sensory overload is extremely low.

Chapter Two: Understanding an Empath

In a world that may often seem like it has gone insane, where we have reached cruelty of immense heights in the name of religion and justice; where there have been far too many genocides to mention, and with slavery in all its forms still existing—empathy is a quality that is seriously lacking. It is the human quality that can solve the cruelties of the world. It enables us to have compassion and respect for one another. It opens our hearts to others and encourages acceptance and understanding of others. It is our pathway towards peace, and therefore becomes vitally important that we recognize it, value it and learn how to best use this gift. To do this, we need to take a deeper understanding of what it means to be an empath.

Empathy vs. Empaths

The first step in doing that is to distinguish empathy from empaths. As stated before empathy is the ability to relate to, understand and share the feelings of someone else. Basically, you can empathize with someone going through a rough time, or you can be genuinely happy for someone who has just achieved something. Empaths can feel these emotions more purely and genuinely. It affects them on a much deeper and real level. There is no filter whether it is joy or sadness. Empaths feel things before they think—which is different from how the rest of society operates. It may be a little difficult to process because we are a society that promotes intellect and rationalization. Because thinking does not happen first, there is no barrier or defense for empaths, they feel everything. This can go to the extreme, where empaths cannot distinguish another person's emotions from their own.

Measuring the Sensitivity of Empaths

Understanding where you fit in the spectrum of empathy is important; because it affects the way you view and interact with the world. There is an exhaustive list of tests that empaths can take to measure their sensitivity. These are intensely interesting to peruse and are quite varied. They vary from questionnaires, reactivity indexes, empathy scales, listening tests, reading emotions tests, and yawning tests—sometimes referred to as the contagious yawning test. The thinking behind the yawning test is that the first person to mimic the yawn is the most empathic of the group.

These tests are usually carried out by trained personnel and can take the form of online, written, observation, and peer assessments. There is also a wide range of self-tests that one can take to get a bit more clarity on which part of the spectrum they fall. Theorists behind these tests date back to 1934 and include the likes of Piaget. Researches look at who is qualified to administer the various tests and how that would affect the outcomes. They need to consider how one can measure empathy and if so, what unit of measurement should be used.

It is interesting to note that there are many tests that are specifically designed for doctors to take to measure their empathy. It is an ability that is needed in order to empathize with ill people. The '*Carkhuff and Truax Empathy Scale*' was designed by Dustin K. MacDonald and is cited below:

"Level 1: Low Level of Empathic Responding
Communicating little or no awareness or understanding of the caller's feelings
Responses are irrelevant or abrasive
Changing the subject, giving advice, etc.

Level 2: Moderately Low Level of Empathic Responding
Responding to the surface message of the caller but omitting feelings or factual aspects of the message.

Inappropriately qualifying feelings (e.g., "somewhat," "a little bit, "kind of")
Inaccurately interpreting feelings (e.g., "angry," "hurt," "tense," or "scared").
Level 2 responses are only partially accurate, but they show an effort to understand.

Level 3: Interchangeable or Reciprocal Level of Empathic Responding
Verbal and nonverbal responses at level 3 show understanding and are essentially interchangeable with the client's obvious expressions, accurately reflecting the client's story and surface feelings or state of being.

Level 4: Moderately High Level of Empathic Responding
Somewhat additive, accurately identifying the client's implicit underlying feelings and/or aspects of the problem.
Volunteer's response illuminates subtle or veiled facets of the client's message, enabling the client to get in touch with somewhat deeper feelings and unexplored meanings and purposes of behavior.
Level 4 responses thus are aimed at enhancing self-awareness.

Level 5: High Level of Empathic Responding
Reflecting each emotional nuance, and using voice and intensity of expressions finely attuned to the client's moment-by-moment experiencing, the volunteer accurately responds to the full range and intensity of both surface and underlying feelings and meanings
A volunteer may connect current feelings and experiencing to previously expressed experiences or feelings, or may accurately identify implicit patterns, themes, or purposes.
Responses may also identify implicit goals embodied in the client's message, which point out a promising direction for personal growth and pave the way for action.

Responding empathically at this high level facilitates the client's exploration of feelings and problems in much greater breadth and depth than responding at a lower level"

Types of Empaths

There are different types of empaths that each portrays a particular strength. The number of types of empaths varies according to the study, article, or doctor. We will look at three of the most common types. While there may be one particular type that you gravitate towards, you can also identify with some aspects of the others. A general understanding of all the types will help you understand how empaths engage and react to the world around them. There are generally three categories which most empaths can fall into. These are the *Physical Empaths*, the *Emotional Empaths*, and the *Intuitive Empaths*.

Physical Empaths

Physical Empaths tend to relate to other people's physical indicators and absorb them into their bodies. They can either be drained or energized by the other person. These empaths usually become healers of some kind, as they use their ability to sense what is wrong with the other person. Physical empaths need to learn how to control their own energy fields so that they can turn it off when dealing with ailments.

Emotional Empaths
Similarly, Emotional Empaths connect with other people's emotions and absorb them, whether they are joyful or sorrowful. This is one of the most common types of empaths that you will find. For these empaths, it is important to distinguish between one's own emotion and that of others.

Intuitive Empaths
Intuitive Empaths are by far the most interesting. They have amazing super senses like telepathy, intuition, interpreting messages through dreams, synchronicity with nature and one of the increasing popular empaths are the Medium Empaths, who have the ability to connect with the other side. These empaths are finely tuned in with the environment and can read people's energy.

Understanding which type of empath, you or your loved one is can help you prevent feeling drained or exhausted and also help you to make the most of your abilities.

How Empaths Interact with Others
Empaths will react to and with the world in different ways, depending on whether they are introverted or extroverted. Introverts are generally considered shy people because they are

more involved with their own ideas and emotions rather than with external matters. And similarly, introverted empaths do not have a high threshold for socializing with large groups of people or for the sake of. They prefer the company of people they know and need an exit strategy as they can feel overstimulated after some time. Introverted empaths need to find ways to slow down and re-center.

In contrast, extroverts are socially confident and outgoing people. Extrovert empaths, by nature, are more focused on external matters. They are more vocal and engaging than their introverted counterparts. They enjoy socializing and being around people. These situations do not exhaust or overstimulate them.

Advantages of Being an Empath

Intuition – being intuitive with the flow of energy of people and nature allows one to feel things fully and be totally immersed in experiencing life.

Compassion – empaths are the most considerate and thoughtful people you will find. They are always ready to help others. They dream of the perfect future.

Creative – most empaths are so in tune with themselves that they are able to be creative and see more than others.

Loyalty – empaths make the best friends as they are fiercely loyal and it would take a lot for them to give up on someone.

Nature – empaths are synchronized with nature. Being surrounded by water rejuvenates them. They form special bonds with animals and often rescue them.

Disadvantages of Being an Empath

Overstimulation – empaths feel exhaustion more easily if they do not take time out for themselves. They easily suffer from sensory overload.

Absorbing negativity – empaths relate to the feelings of others so closely that it becomes difficult to differentiate their feelings from those of others. This can cause emotional or physical symptoms to manifest in them.

Compassion – the ability to feel things so closely to those of others can also be a disadvantage. Negative things of this world can be difficult to shake off and can bring them down. They feel the full weight of the pain and suffering of others.

Over stimulation – experiencing sensory overload can take time to get over.

Loneliness –sometimes empaths feel the need to be alone so often that they tend to isolate people from their lives. They may come across as being anti-social when they are trying to look out for themselves.

Exploitation – sometimes people can take advantage of the giving and compassionate nature of empaths.

Sensory overload – coping with loud people, business, noises, and smells can be very daunting for people, whereas some empaths are energized by the full moon, or snowfalls, or thunderstorms.

Expressing needs – needs of intimate relationships can be difficult to articulate. In intimate relationships, not all partners can appreciate an empaths' need for space, or not wanting to share a bed.

Hopefully, this chapter has given you a greater insight into what it means to be an empath.

Chapter Three: How to Have Healthy Relationships

Despite all that we have said thus far about some empaths not being able to be around people for long periods of time, it is possible for empaths to enjoy healthy, positive, and intimate relationships with others. The right balance in a relationship can actually be empowering to empaths. But as always, there are certain things that they need to be aware of to avoid unhealthy dynamics in relationships.

Challenges That Empaths Face in Intimate Relationships

Many empaths will admit to wanting to be a recluse at times. Sometimes they need to be alone like they need to breathe and this can be very hurtful to a partner. As a result, many empaths avoid getting into relationships and remain single for most of their lives. However, being an empath does not mean that one has to relegate themselves to the abyss of loneliness or have a series of short-term relationships. Once you recognize that you are an empath and understand the emotions you feel, as well as why you are feeling them, you can find ways to create the harmony and balance you seek. You will know how to protect yourself from others and not get lost in a relationship or have to endure traumatic relationships. We will deal with ways to protect yourself later in *Chapter Seven*.

Being with someone for long periods of time can be overwhelming to an empath. As much as you may want to experience the joy of being in a relationship, it can get a bit too much. Many empaths run for the hills and leave relationships when this happens. Not recognizing your needs as an empath can make one feel suffocated in relationships and lead to its destruction. Being an empath does not have to mean being alone, it just means that you and your partner will need to adjust to your particular needs. Recognizing the need for an alone time by both partners can lead to a beautiful love experience. This time will refill you and ultimately enhance the relationship and not take away from it. It is important that this time apart is not taken personally, because it is rather paradoxical, you have a need to feel loved and have companionship but are also afraid of being engulfed and overwhelmed by the relationship. Many empaths unknowingly circumvent getting into relationships because this aspect of absorbing energies and emotions are not understood and result in solitude. Recognizing the need to take care of yourself in a relationship is very important to the sustainability of any relationship.

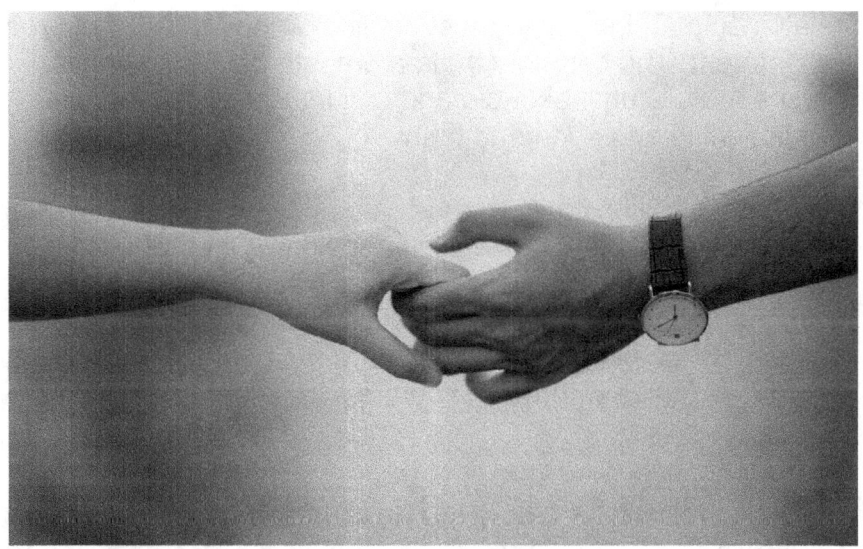

Being honest about your 'energy' needs is crucial to the longevity of a relationship. If one is not verbal about these needs, it will eventually become unbearable. The empath will seek a space of little to no stimulation, preferably in nature somewhere, before feeling comfortable within themselves again. Setting boundaries and understanding the energy needs of an empath gives intimate relationships potential. In some cases, traditional models of coupledom may have to change, it all depends on the specific space and time apart—needs that an empath requires. This varies according to personalities, upbringing, culture, and environment.

Empaths are very good at recognizing and expressing their feelings quicker than others. This can be very daunting in a relationship and make them seem like "*know it all's*" and breed resentment. The certainty that an empath has about what he/she feels is unshakeable and can lead to arguments in relationships and even end them.

Empaths can also come across as being very temperamental because everything they feel is intensified, whether it is joy or anger. Empaths will pick up when a person is lying or not being true to their feelings and will be quite vocal about this not to cause conflict, but because they care. All of these aspects can be difficult to live with when you are in a close relationship.

Why Empaths Make the Best Partners

Embarking on a long-term relationship with an empath can be daunting and filled with challenges from the onset. But let's face it, which relationships are all roses? All relationships require work, effort, and sacrifices for them to progress. However, being in a relationship with an empath can be one of the most rewarding experiences one can have. If scientifically, we know that the empaths' brains are designed to discern the emotions and thoughts of others, then they are the best people to truly and fully understand their partners. Loyalty, compassion, respect, care, love, and understanding will come in leaps and bounds; respecting, understanding, and accepting the needs of an empath can transform a relationship into one full of devotion and mutual love towards each other.

Reasons to Be in a Relationship with an Empath

Empaths are natural healers and caregivers.
They do it for the joy it brings to others and in return feel that joy. Empaths cannot tolerate people experiencing pain; they will do what they can to ease it.

Empaths are fiercely loyal to the people they love and trust.
They will go through leaps and bounds for the other person to make them feel loved and content.

Empaths can spread joy and happiness.
This can infect the people that they are surrounded by. Being in a loving relationship will exponentially increase this sense of joy which in turn will spread to their partners.

Empaths extremely genuine about what they say and do.
Being wired to sense feelings and thoughts make them that way. Because of this, empaths love unconditionally and understand the needs of their partners.

Empathic people have empathy!
Instead of being angry and reacting, they will try to understand, this makes them far more loving and peaceful in nature.

Empaths are natural optimists.
It is a survival strategy against all the negativity of the world. Being with an empath means you will always get to see the brighter side of things.

Empaths have the innate ability to inspire others and change the world.

They can affect positive change the partners that they are in a relationship with.

Empaths are so in tune with emotions and feelings.
Because of that, they are honest and open about them. This gives an empath's partner security in knowing where they stand. An empath will not play games with someone's emotions and will always be kind and thoughtful.

Empaths are creative because they are so in tune with the world.
This makes them good at solving problems and finding solutions for people and situations.

Empaths are able to connect with others on a much deeper level.
They are so in tune with energies and feelings to the point where they are unable to distinguish it from their own. Being in a relationship with an empath will mean that you will always be understood.

Once an empath falls in love with a person it will be unconditionally.
They will accept all the failings as well as the merits of that person.

For those empaths that still feel that they should shy away from intimate relationships, it must be noted that coupledom is not for everyone. So instead of sabotaging potential relationships, it is better to understand and accept this.

Dealing with Family and Friends
Intimate relationships are not the only kinds of relationships that empaths struggle with. They can struggle with friendships and with family members as well. Personal space needs to be recognized and negotiated depending on the nature of the relationship. In public spaces, not having enough personal space can be suffocating to an empath. Empaths can find

creative ways to keep the physical distance from others, like using your trolley in queues so that people don't get too close or putting your handbag on the seat next to you so that no one sits there. With friends and family, it can be a little trickier. You have to ensure that you don't offend anyone. To do this, you must be clear that it is not about not loving them and not a personal thing. Being able to articulate these needs will go a long way to creating lasting relationships, rather than you pulling disappearing acts every time you feel emotionally drained. Once you identify the emotional boundary you need, communicating it to others will be much easier. Your relationships with others will flourish and you will not have to feel smothered and avoid them. This negotiation will benefit all parties involved.

Empaths and Narcissists

Firstly, an *empath* is someone who feels an innate need to help and heal others. A *narcissist* is someone who cannot put the needs of others first and are very self-involved. As a result, a narcissist and an empath can often result in toxic relationships. However, narcissists and empaths do have a lot in common. They both recognize the emotional needs and motivations of people. This gives them insight into the insecurities of people. A narcissist will use this information to their own gains whereas an empath will use this information to try and help the other person. So, it is easy to see how this will not bode well in a relationship.

The truth is that many narcissists and empaths are drawn to each other because they reflect each other's vices. An empath struggles with feeling dismissed and lost, while a narcissist struggles with obligation and weakness. Empaths, who do not understand themselves fully, will enter these relationships because they believe that love will conquer all. They give off themselves selflessly and to their own detriment. They have no boundaries and become emotionally dependent on the narcissist. Narcissists are often not in touch with their feelings and lack empathy; they would rather see this as a weakness that must be controlled. Narcissists, therefore, seek out empaths as the means through which they can express themselves.

This does not mean that narcissists and empaths should never enter relationships with each other. If the empath recognizes and sets boundaries, there will not be room for a narcissist to manipulate and abuse them. Narcissists need to be forced to deal with and recognize their feelings, and they will start to deal with the root cause of the problem, rather than just project their feelings onto others. The most important thing for narcissists and empaths in a relationship is to be aware of themselves and manage and control their own feelings and behaviors and avoid blaming each other. Being aware of and accepting one's vices will transform into positive aspects, and this awareness can propel narcissists and empaths into productive and progressive relationships. They can then use their high emotional intelligence to realize their potential and live full, happy lives.

Relationship Advice for Empaths

Being in a mutually respectful and loving relationship is important so we have some advice for an empath embarking on this journey.

It is important to express the need for your emotional and personal space early on in the relationship. If the person understands this need, then it bodes well for the relationship. However, if the person puts you down for expressing this need, then the warning bells should go off. The need for space can take different forms, sometimes it can just be a stroll around the block by yourself, other times it could be a weekend getaway—alone.

Some empaths cannot share a bed with a partner. A potential partner needs to understand this need for uninterrupted space and not see it as a rejection of any sort. Energies will mix when sleeping, so to some empaths, this can cause restless sleep. Partners need to understand this and let go of the traditional pattern of coupledom. For some relationships, this could mean sleeping in separate rooms or sleeping apart for a few nights or just separate beds in the same room.

It is crucial for empaths to be honest about their anxieties and what they feel. This will aid in any misunderstandings and can bring couples closer together, as well as allow the partner to play a supportive role. Just as much as an empath needs to be heard, they should also listen to their partners. This way, compromises can be made—if needed—and will create the emotional freedom that healthy relationships need.

Chapter Four: How to Be a Parent as an Empath

It can be particularly challenging for empaths to be parents. Since they absorb everything that their child feels, it can leave them feeling exhausted. Raising empathic children can also be overwhelming. They do not fully understand their sensitivities yet. There are guidelines and techniques to help parents who are raising empaths, to ensure all children are nurtured and developed to their fullest capabilities.

Parenting

If empaths connect so deeply with people's feeling and emotions, can you imagine the extent that this would go to with their own children? Children of empaths would probably have the best childhoods ever. Children of empaths feel loved, taken care of, supported, and heard. Their parents are very much in tune with how they feel and what they need. Parenting as an empath can be a very different experience. Imagine absorbing every emotion of your child? Feeling anxious when they cry, feeling pain when they are rejected, the stress of not wanting them to be hurt in any way, and wanting to protect them from the world. This can lead to significant stress levels.
Being attuned to your offspring puts you on super alert to everything they feel. Sometimes it is worse for you than them. Emotions can sway from the broodiness of teenagers to the hyper-activeness of toddlers. This rollercoaster is enough to send any parent over the edge—but so much more so for empathic parents. The weight of carrying all those emotions can sit on you for a long time. It seems like there is no escape and that as a parent, all the responsibility lies within you. Empathic parents blame themselves for being too involved and are accused of being too anxious and worrying too much. You either admire or look at other parents in horror by how laid back they

may be. Empathic parents are often *'burned out'* and exhausted. The good news is that empathic parents are more likely to raise healthier and happier children and that there are ways to protect yourself from *'burning out'*.

Some characteristics of parents that are empaths are hyper-vigilance and stress. While to some this may seem like an anxiety disorder, it stems from concern for one's child. Being super aware of potential dangers can be exhausting and can also make you seem tense. This long-term stress is not good for the body, mind, and soul. Constantly putting your children's needs before your own can leave you mentally, emotionally, and physically fatigued.

Despite the automatic urge to constantly put your children first, you have to learn how to stop doing that. You have to learn how to take care of yourself first so that you can be your best for them. The basic foundation is to develop emotional resilience. Research shows that you can do this in three ways:

You have to learn how to be calm.
The minute you trigger stress by worrying about your child, you need to stop and breathe. This activates your parasympathetic nervous system, which counters the sympathetic nervous

system—our stress response. When you feel nervous, you start to breathe faster. When you consciously slow your breathing down, your body gets all the signals to calm itself. Inhaling increases your heart rate, exhaling decreases the heart rate. So by lengthening the time between breaths will slow your heart rate, and in turn, calm you down.

Develop self-compassion.
The next step is one of the most underutilized of techniques. Developing self-compassion will improve your physical and psychological well-being. Self-compassion can give you strength. It involves being kind to yourself. Less self-criticism and more kindness are needed. We need to remind ourselves that no one needs to be perfect and that everyone makes mistakes. We can give comfort and encouragement easily to others, but not necessarily ourselves. Basically, we need to use more empathy on ourselves. Being mindful of your thoughts and feelings will help to stand back from it and look at them objectively. This way you don't have to give in to a flood of emotions or deny them.

Give yourself some alone time.
The third step has been touched on earlier in the chapter—alone time. Empaths need this time to rejuvenate themselves. Separation from your children may seem counter-intuitive and even painful, but it is necessary. This can be as simple as taking a relaxing bath, reading a book or taking a walk by yourself.

It is important to practice all these techniques regularly to avoid mental and emotional fatigue. Practice will make regulating intense feelings easier to do. It will also strengthen the emotional resilience you need to flourish as a parent. This, in turn, will filter to your child, making them feel even more secure. The most important thing to remember is to keep the balance between self-care and enjoying the feeling of relating so closely to your offspring.

Nurturing Empathic Children

You do not have to be an empath to give birth to empathic children. And you do not have to be an empath to raise healthy, balanced, empathic children. Just like how adult empaths sense and feel things so intensely, so do empathic children. The difficulty is that children do not know yet how to handle the emotions they feel, so this becomes exponentially more difficult for empathic children. Their nervous systems react more intensely to external stimuli which can lead to sensory overload very quickly. They may respond more intensely to certain smells, bright lights, and noisy spaces. They may prefer certain perfumes, softer fabrics, being in nature etc. Empathic parents can help these children identify triggers and provide solutions to these emotions since they are not able to express or understand the intensity themselves. This will help them deal with it and minimize any discomfort.

As parents of empathic children, you need to know your children well. You need to know what over stimulates them and how to prevent those situations. This will help keep them calm, relaxed, and avoid tantrums. Some common triggers for empathic children are:
- Keeping them busy, filling their days with tasks and activities with no breaks
- Violent programs particularly at night
- Multi-tasking
- No time alone or apart from others

When exposed to the above situations, you may find it harder to get your child to fall asleep. They may need more time to unwind. Parents of empathic children need to remember that their children do not have the same ability to filter out noise, light, and chaos, unlike other children. They may cry or confine themselves to solitude. Certain stimuli can even be painful to them, like cheering and clapping. These sounds will disturb them as opposed to the calming sounds of water and nature.

As much as there are scientific evidence and research, many schools are not equipped to identify or understand empathic children. They are often labeled as anti-social, shy, or fussy. Their quiet, compassionate, and deep nature can give the impression that they are just reserved. In extreme cases, they get diagnosed with a disorder, depression, anxiety, or phobias. It is important for parents to arm themselves with knowledge and solutions in order to help environments like schools make life easier for empathic children. Combatting these misperceptions with tools and awareness will help empathic children and their caregivers cope with the world.

Parents and caregivers should also remember that these children feel and absorb the joy and pain of those around them and can experience emotional discomfort from these situations. Whatever the adult feels, it will be intensified for the child.

There are many people who do not understand what empaths are, let alone how to respond to them. When empathic children are dismissed as being 'overly sensitive' and told to 'grow thicker skin' they are made to feel like there is something wrong with them. They will feel misunderstood and start to withdraw from people. It is important for us to increase the awareness and support of empathic children in understanding their unique qualities.

How to Know If Your Child Is an Empath?

Recognizing whether or not your child is an empath is the first step to helping your child live the best that they can be. Once this is established, a parent can support them in the way that is required. Below are some traits of empathic children:

- They have intense emotions.
- They get quickly over-stimulated when they are around crowds and noise.
- They have strong reactions to sad books or scary movies.
- They often want to leave family gatherings early or just be by themselves.
- They think they are different from other children.
- They are very good at listening to people.
- They amaze you with intuitive or insightful comments that you would not expect from a child.

- They have a particular affinity for nature and animals.
- They get upset when other children have been mistreated or victimized.
- They have a few good friends, rather than a large circle of friends.

The more your child can relate, the stronger their empathic inclinations are. It is important to nurture these children as they have the abilities needed to solve the cruel world we live in. they need to learn to appreciate their sensitivities and nor resent them.

Chapter Five: How to Thrive in the World of Work as an Empath

One of the things we spent a huge amount of time doing is our jobs or occupations. Finding the right job for an empath is like the difference between a happy fulfilled life and a frustrated one. Privacy is difficult to get in many work environments with many open-plan office spaces. Being constantly surrounded by people can leave an empath feeling very overwhelmed. It is important, especially for empaths, to find environments that suit their temperament or learn how to set boundaries and learn how to center themselves at work.
Empaths are naturally driven to make the world a better place. They share a strong desire to help people and often sacrifice themselves in the process. It is, therefore, important for empaths to find work that is meaningful to them, that will make a positive impact on the lives of others. They tend to stay away from competitive careers and those driven by money. Careers in the healing field like teaching and counseling appeal more to empaths.

A Changing Work Environment
It is becoming an increasing ten in the workplace for empaths to be placed on emotional quotient, rather than intelligence quotient. Humanity or empathy is becoming more of a priority, as well as a social responsibility. It seems that empaths are starting to make their mark on the world after all.
Companies that can develop an empathic culture are the ones that thrive. When you can step into someone else's shoes and relate to them genuinely, they feel appreciated and give so much more and are much more loyal. Empaths can offer much to the work environment because they genuinely care; however, if they do not protect themselves, they can succumb to exhaustion and feeling overwhelmed. More empaths are needed in the workplace. Research shows that productivity is on

the decline when employees feel that their managers do not care about them and the work that they do. Workers feel that their employers are out of touch with what happens on the ground and remain aloof in the confinement of boardrooms and presentations.

Emotional contagion was discussed earlier in the book. One can see how dangerous this could be to a work environment. It can affect the morale of the staff if it is negative. However, the opposite can be said if it is a positive, happy, and productive work environment.

In today's work environments, there is not much space between co-workers, so it makes it difficult for an empath to avoid the stimulation from others. An empath can hear others around them gossiping, complaining, coughing, and laughing. They can smell the odors of the people around them. This sensory overload can be hugely stressful to empaths.

Some progressive companies have recognized the need of their employees and provide creative and alternative spaces for their employees to perform at their best. You now find couches in some workplaces, designated quiet spaces for those that need it.

It is not always possible to control the environment you find yourself in, but you can learn some techniques to help you cope. There are ways to minimize emotional contagion and to create a safe, pleasant workspace for yourself. The first thing you need to do is understand energy.

There are colleagues who will energize empaths, and there are colleagues who will make empaths feel like they suck the life out of them. The relationship you have with these people will ultimately affect your physical well-being. It is important to thrive in a working environment where you can recognize these different types of people and learn how to navigate your way around them to prevent fatigue and resentment. It is important to create an environment where you can feel safe and happy.

Empaths need to limit the time they set aside to listen to other people, especially if these are mainly complaints. It helps to have exit lines ready to use like "*I'm sorry, I have many deadlines to meet today, I only have a few minutes to spare*" or politely change the topic. Some co-workers do not respond to verbal or nonverbal cues, and you have to approach the problem more directly. It is important to recognize any triggers and respond calmly and rationally. If these do not work, you can try visualization—putting yourself in a happier more serene space where the negativity the co-worker brings does not affect you. By looking at the people you need to be in contact with and the ways that they affect you, you can find strategies to help you deal with them. Setting limits and implementing them is the key when it comes to people who will upset your emotional well-being.

A workplace can either drain all your energy and motivation away or energize and nourish you. Obviously, it is the latter we all aspire to, as it will create an environment that fosters creativity and passion. The former will probably find an empath staying away from work, feeling sick often, and constantly feel emotional stress.

Since work and careers play such a momentous part of our lives, it is important to create the right environment. Achieving this is twofold, you have to find meaning and purpose in your job, and you have to understand and manage the energy of the space and people around you.

Understanding Energy

Everything on earth has its own vibration and therefore its own energy. For empaths, energy becomes a primary means of communication. Plants, animals, people, and even water have a vibration or frequency that is unique to it. This is what defines their existence in the universe. This knowledge is based on scientific evidence that is documented. You can actually see these vibrations and frequencies in brain scans and other energy graphs.

Negative energy attracts more negative energy and positive attracts positive energy. Energy can also repel each other. Empaths and non-empaths can consciously use this energy if they are aware of it. Some people send out positive energy and you feel refreshed around them. Other people absorb positive energy and leave people around them feeling drained. The minute one starts to pay attention to this aspect, you will notice it more and more. There are some people that are just more charismatic and attract you to them. Think about dynamic leaders and how you feel after being in their presence.

An empath is affected by the energy that is emitted from others. People may not be aware of the emotional frequencies that they send out. When an empath picks up on this, they will have an emotional or physical response to it. The more enlightened you are as an empath, the quicker and easier it is to do this. An untrained empath is vulnerable to these and will be affected more intensely. Walking into a boardroom or networking session can easily turn into a nightmare for empaths. They may feel overwhelmed and struggle to concentrate and focus. Empaths need to become aware of the people that feed off their energy, this can happen in the first moments of coming into contact with that person. This difference in energy needs can lead to stress and a breakdown in the relationship. Highly stressful situations at work can be avoided if empaths learn how to block the emotions or energies that they are feeling. Most of the time, people are unaware of their energy frequencies and do not realize the effect it has on others. It is important for empaths to train themselves on how to cope with various situations and predicaments, and thereby, shield themselves from unnecessary and debilitating stress.

Creating Boundaries

It is important to create physical and emotional boundaries around yourself at work. Not all of us have the mental fortitude of gurus and monks, so the good news is that empaths can also use some physical objects in their environment to help them in this regard. These may serve more as a psychological barrier, but it will help with your state of mind.

If you find yourself in a modern-day open plan office space, where you do not enjoy the space that your desk provides, you can create a type of barrier around you.
By this, I mean a physical barrier with small plants, photos or precious stones.
Create emotional distance from people by using earphones that cut off sound and noise.
You can take breaks or a walk to get fresh air.
You can also purify a place by burning scented candles or incense. However, you have to be aware that some co-workers may be uncomfortable with this.
You could do a silent meditation that is not invasive to anyone. And finally, you can use objects like plants and mirrors to change the energy of the space.

Visualization helps some people. You visualize that your entire workspace is surrounded by light that resists anything negative and only attracts that which is positive. It is a strategy to help you feel protected, and thereby, empower you.

Empaths need to learn how to cope with negative people in the workplace and use whatever means are at their disposal to aid them. How you cope with this at work can affect your comfort levels at work. One has to learn and practice strategies to create the physical, emotional and psychological barriers that are required to create a pleasant work environment. You may not be able to control who you work with, or even the setting you work in, but you can try at shifting the energy you find yourself in. you can use the above strategies to minimize the emotional contagion found in workspaces.

Choosing Careers
When an empath finds the right career for them, they can be invaluable in that field. An empath needs to recognize that their

contributions may not be valued in certain fields like the military or corporations, but highly sought after in fields of healthcare, education, and the arts. When choosing a career, an empath needs to consider not just the requirements and skills of a job but also the energy of the environment, and the vision and mission of the company. An empath will need to trust their intuition and instinct when it comes to making a decision, as this requires actively being aware of the energy they sense.

The key factor when choosing a career path is to truly understand and know your capabilities. Compassionate professions can be an excellent career choice initially, but the weight of carrying the pain and the suffering of others can be too much to bear. Trained empaths who can set boundaries, coping techniques, and limits can strive in these fields. Knowing who you are, and your limits will help you make the best career choice for you.

The Best Jobs for Empaths

There are certain fields that are naturally inclined towards the best traits of an empath and will provide them with fulfillment and satisfaction.

Many empaths are natural artists. An artist's job is to reflect the world they find themselves in, or comment on it and make others contemplate these ideas, and because empaths are more perceptive and in tune with their environment, they are naturally inclined towards being an artist. The intensity with which they feel and sense the world helps them in creating meaningful art in all forms. Empaths, who choose a field of art, find a way to channel whatever they feel into their art. In return, the world is beautified by these wonderful expressions that move us and inspire us. There are very few artists in the world that get rich by creating their art, so the motivation behind this is more to make an impact on the world and change lives for the better.

Healthcare

The compassionate and caring nature of an empath makes them ideal for an occupation in healthcare. Many empaths become doctors, nurses, and psychologists to fill their need to help others. The most important thing for empaths, as healthcare professionals, is to have techniques and strategies to shield them from taking on too much from their patients.

Social workers deal directly with vulnerable people and children—empaths would naturally gravitate towards this career. They give their time and effort and often work long hours. Their goal is to improve and protect the lives of the people they come into contact with. This career, however, can expose an empath to the harsh and cruel realities of the world; it is imperative that they have strong coping strategies to deal with the pain and suffering that they come across. Not having these strategies in place have caused many social workers to leave their jobs after a few years due to emotional and mental exhaustion.

Many empaths find themselves in hospice work where they provide care and support to families of patients with illnesses. They also provide extra care and support to the patient as the families' may not necessarily be able to cope. Some empaths do this type of work as volunteers, as their day jobs may not fill their need to help others.

At first, one may think to be a lawyer is at odds with who an empath is, but it can be a perfect fit for those who need to champion causes. It is a job where you can serve and help people and make a difference in the world. We generally associate lawyers with expensive fees and being ruthless, but this is a generalization and stereotype. Empaths as lawyers can identify with what their clients feel, and what they are going through, this makes them the best people to represent others, especially those that are abused. There are times that the sensitivities of an empath will fair against them in situations when there are huge conflict and great stress.

Self-employment becomes a choice for many empaths as they can have the flexibility and freedom to choose their work environments. They get to choose their colleagues and clients and can work on their own if they feel the need to. Self-employment also means fewer meetings with groups of people, and that is a huge positive for empaths.

Many businesses have opted for flexi-time and allow employees to work from home and communicate via apps and online platforms. This environment is also suitable to empaths. The disadvantage is that one often ends up working far more than they would at an office. So once again, it becomes important to implement boundaries.

The Worst Jobs for Empaths

Sales jobs are probably one of the worst jobs that an empath can try. This job requires one to deal with all kinds of people and manipulate them into purchasing something that you know deep down they do not really need. This is at complete odds for an empath who seeks to help and enhance the lives of others. A sales job can be emotionally draining for an empath. Being a salesperson in a shop or supermarket can mean that an empath is bombarded by people, noises, loudspeakers, and bright lights all the time. This is the exact opposite description of the ideal environment for an empath.

Customer care and public relations may also be very stressful choices for an empath, as they are careers that involve small talk, being aggressive and agreeable. The corporate world presents problems for an empath as well. There is usually rules and protocols to follow that are non-negotiable and do not value the individual. Empaths are deep thinkers and enjoy thinking out of the box to find solutions. They will speak up if they feel strongly about an issue and won't be swayed easily. This ability may not go down well in all corporate environments, and they can be seen as being difficult. They don't do well with competitive co-workers and can find them draining.

If you do find yourself in one of these careers and no way out, you can find ways to improve your situation. Empaths who are happy at work can be valuable employees.

Chapter Six: Why Some Empaths Turn to Addiction

Many people, even those that are mindful of empaths and non-empaths, are unaware that empaths do not have the tools to cope with what the world throws at them. They do not know how to cope with the feeling of being overwhelmed and turn to negative means of coping with these feelings. Empaths will try to solve or numb what they are feeling by turning to addictions. These can take the form of alcohol, medication, sex, gambling, food etc.

Medication is sometimes the easy go-to when empaths feel the sensory overload, which can lead to anxiety and depression. This solution deals with the symptoms and not the cause. Empaths need to learn how to shield themselves from the intensity of their emotions, rather than turning to quick-fix solutions.

Empaths also need to learn to accept themselves and realize that they are different from other people and will not cope in the same ways as other people. These can sometimes refer to things that other people take completely for granted. Going to the supermarket at the end of the month or navigating freeways during peak traffic times, can affect empaths intensely. They can feel extreme anxiety by doing these simple day to day activities. Non-empaths will not understand how these events can cause sensory overload and hyper-stimulation for empaths. Breathing exercises do not always help in these situations, and the lack of empathy and understanding from others and themselves can make empaths turn to alternative means, or ways of dealing with what they feel.

Addiction becomes distractions from having to deal with the sensory overload. It takes your attention away from having to deal with the world. Certain addictive substances like medication and alcohol can change the energy or vibration of an empath, either making it higher or lower, putting them in a state where they are not as aware of the sensory input around them. Addictions to running, exercise, or yoga will release endorphins which counter any pain felt because endorphins are associated with feel-good hormones.

Food becomes another way that empaths numb themselves. Foods high in carbohydrates or sugars raise insulin. It is believed that we crave these foods because they raise our dopamine levels. So, empaths turn to these foods as a way to counter the depression or sensory overload that they feel.

Many addicts come from homes that are supportive and wealthy—which leave people thinking and pondering about why they became addicts. If what the empaths feel is amplified, then those people are carrying loads of emotional pain, anxiety, loss, and hurt of many. This can be debilitating, and it can be difficult to feel upbeat or normal. For the most part, empaths try to keep an emotional balance through alcohol, smoking, and eating addictions, but for others, it is much harder to keep the addiction under control.

For the most part, the addiction is a way to disconnect and to retreat. But no matter how much empaths try to distance themselves from feeling through substances, it does not solve the problem. If anything, it creates more conflicts in our relationships and can cause further frustration, loneliness, and depression. The distance empaths can create can take the following forms:
- Preferring isolation
- Decreased sex drive
- Being emotionally shut off
- Ending relationships

More and more research are beginning to show that the answer to addiction is a connection. By this, I mean that instead of empaths trying to avoid the feelings, they should embrace them fully as a means to release them. One way to do this is by talking about these feelings to someone they trust and that will support. This is the connection!

Medication and Empaths

There are times when trying to deal with the sensory overload can be too overwhelming and medication is needed to combat depression and anxiety. The good news is that since empaths are so sensitive to everything, they are also sensitive to medication, and therefore, require less for it to start showing positive results. Many empaths usually find that traditional doses of medication are difficult for them to tolerate. Many pain medications inhibit empathy and become a go-to drug for empaths who are trying to cope with a barrage of emotions. Empaths, who need medication, need to find medical practitioners who are sensitive to the sensitivity of empaths and can adjust the dosage accordingly.

Chapter Seven: How to Protect Yourself as an Empath

Empaths need to learn ways and means to protect themselves from toxic people, or when they are around noise, business, and chaos to avoid feeling overwhelmed and exhausted. One of the many abilities of empaths is honing in subtle non-verbal cues, thereby opening themselves up to the feelings and energy of others that are not consciously displayed. This makes empaths good at reading people and situations and knowing when people are being dishonest or not authentic. However, the negative side to these abilities is that it presents the empaths with a host of problems. They can be overwhelmed by energy overload, by absorbing other people's energy. Negative energy can leave an empath feeling disconnected and heavy.

We have spoken in previous chapters about boundaries and setting limits and being assertive. In Chapter Five, we covered aspects of psychological, emotional, and physical barriers that empaths can use to protect themselves. This chapter sums up all the things an empath can do proactively to reduce this sensory onslaught and techniques to get rid of it.

Energy Fields

Every person has invisible sheets of electromagnetic waves that surround them, some people refer to this as their aura, but a more scientific term is *'biofield'*. For non-empaths, this field is well defined and unified. For empaths, it is permeable and fluid. This makes it vulnerable to the penetration of foreign energy. Trained empaths can use this sensitivity to read spaces and people. They can sense when they walk into a room or space and immediately feel if it is tense or welcoming. Places where there is a lot of energy condensed together like shopping malls, schools, and hospitals offer energy overload to empaths and they try to avoid them. As an empath, one has to learn about how energy works, as well as your own personal sensitivities and the type of empath you are. This information will help guide you to the techniques and tools you will need.

Taking Care of Yourself

There are certain rituals that an empath needs to follow to avoid all the negative stuff they are prone to. The first is the little things that they need to do to take care of themselves. Empaths need to be in tune with their vibrations, as it creates the foundation from which they interact with the world. Non-empaths are attracted to the high vibrations of empaths and see them as role models. In this way, empaths can teach others how to be in this world and eliminate many cruelties. When empaths take care of and look after themselves, they will teach others, by example, to do the same. By taking care of themselves first, empaths will be able to blossom and fulfill their purpose in this life, and thereby, make an impact on the world.

Healthy Living

The first step in this process is to look at what we put into our bodies, on our bodies, and what we surround our bodies with. Things we put into our bodies include *food, medication, and drinks*.
Things we put on our bodies include *clothing, jewelry, etc.*
Things we surround ourselves with include *furniture, household items, even cleaning products*.
All of these things will have an effect on our bodies, and empaths will be more susceptible to its influence. Being aware of the choices an empath makes when purchasing all of these various items must be careful and deliberate. Generally, these items should be organic. Non-organic items have a lower vibration and can negatively affect empaths. Being extremely sensitive means, that empaths must make conscious choices.

Exercise

We release toxins from our bodies through salt. So when empaths cry or sweat, it is actually very good for them. Toxins and negative energy will build up in the body over time, so it is important to release these on a regular basis. If you do not like exercising, you can find creative ways to sweat. Many gyms now offer heated studios for yoga and Pilates. Yoga is designed to release negative energy through meditation, so the combination with sweating makes it an excellent choice. Biking, walking, or running in nature is also very good. Nature has a vibration and can heal you.

Meditation

A great way to clear your mind, discharging negative energy, and reconnecting with yourself is through meditation. Meditation is crucial for empaths, so we have dedicated the entire next chapter to meditation. Meditation does not have to be long and onerous; it can be adapted to the needs and situation. Some empaths prefer to meditate in yoga or outdoors in nature, some prefer guided meditation, and some just prefer to focus on their breathing; for some, it is just some alone time, a place where they can be still. Whichever form appeals to you is the one you should go for. The most important thing is to do it on a regular basis. Quick meditations throughout the day can help an empath stay centered. If an empath feels that their heartbeat is increasing, or a sense of fear and being overwhelmed, they should stop and do a quick meditation to bring them back in charge of their emotional state. These short meditations should not be underestimated, they can be phenomenal.

Good Judgment

Empaths must learn to make good choices. They need to make conscious choices about who they spend their time with, how they spend their time, and where they spend their time. If these choices do not support their purpose in life or higher good, they will not be beneficial to anyone else. An empath can use their gut feelings or intuition to guide them in this regard. When authentic choices are made, toxicity and overload can be eliminated.

Listening to Your Instincts
As has been stated throughout this book, empaths are extremely sensitive. This means being in tune with their senses can make them intuitive. Empaths need to learn how to listen, understand and interpret what their instincts, feelings, and senses are telling them. To do this, empaths need to be very aware of how their bodies respond in different situations. Their intuition will tell them if their energy has increased or decreased when in certain situations or around certain people. With practice, this becomes easier and quicker. To begin with, an empath will have to make a conscious effort to be aware of this intuition or feeling. Then it is important to follow this instinct and stick to people who increase your energy and limit the time you spend with people who decrease your energy. Sometimes intuition can come in the form of dreams, ideas, and thoughts. Intuition will provide signs and guidance but no an explanation. Expressing gratitude also helps an empath to keep at the moment. Expressing gratitude on a regular basis will also increase the positive energy around you.

Spiritual Guidance
Having a spiritual connection provides an opportunity for empaths to experience support, understanding, and unconditional love. This spiritual connection can take any form that is suitable and comfortable for the empath. For some its guardian angels, for some it's prayer. Developing this connection will provide healing and clarity. This connection can even take place during meditations.

Breathing
Mindful breathing is very closely related to meditation. It is basically becoming aware of your breath. You can use this to breathe in positive energy and breathe out negative energy. You will feel the difference in your heart rate and feel calmer. This can be practiced throughout the day and whenever you feel you are in a stressful situation.

A Time Out
This aspect has been covered previously in the book. It is essential to empaths and a deliberate effort to taking time out has to be made. These little breaks of alone time will help to emotionally unwind. A timeout can be as long as you want. It can be an entire weekend away or just a quick walk by oneself.

Some Tips on How to Keep Centered
Empaths are more affected by negative influences than non-empaths. Setting boundaries and sticking to them is vital to your emotional health. It is okay to say "No" to someone if you feel they are asking too much of you. It is okay to put distance between yourself and anything that brings your energy down. Empaths need to do whatever it requires to keep their peace of mind. This may mean limiting one's contact with anything negative—even watching the news or watching horrific and violent programs.
If you know you will be exposed to large groups of people or crowds and you cannot avoid them, plan exit strategies like going to your car or having another means of transportation. Set a limit to the time you will spend there. This should be based on your comfort levels. It helps to eat a high protein meal before the time. This will ground you. You can also stay closer to the perimeter or quieter areas and avoid being in the dead center of a space.
Try not to eat to numb what you are feeling. When feeling tempted, practice a quick meditation and exercise caution. It also helps to have something near the refrigerator to help remind you in case you unwittingly find yourself at your refrigerator ready to indulge.
You can't always shake off and avoid emotions. Sometimes they need to be addressed. Empaths

can learn to manage their emotions by recognizing them and delving into the causes and associations with them. Have honest, realistic conversations with yourself to put these thoughts and feelings into perspective. Realizing where they come from can allow you to recognize them as true feelings, or perhaps there is another way to look at it and minimize your stress.

Develop a routine of cleaning and clearing your spaces. Pay particular attention to your spaces at home and at work, where you would spend most of your time. People turn towards sprays, oils, incense, sage, and feng shui to clear the energy fields around them. This routine should include yoga and other forms of exercise as well.

It is important to learn how to recognize what your needs are. Empaths are generally very sensitive so they need to be aware of the environments that they may find exhausting. They need to be aware of environments where they feel refreshed and rejuvenated. Mastering the balance of the two will enable an empath to function at their best. Empaths need to honor what they need, be it time for contemplation or healing.

It helps to associate with people that are aware and sensitive to the needs of an empath. They can be a support system and help to implement and remind you of the techniques or means you have at your disposal when required.

Taking care of yourself in this way will help you to be better for your friends and family and be a source of joy, comfort, and healing to them.

Tips to Renounce Toxic Energy

Being an empath can be difficult at first. Even if we do practice pro-active regimes to avoid taking on toxic energy, it can still

happen. There are things that an empath can do if this does happen.
Here are some tips:

> The first thing to do is to evaluate whether what you are feeling actually does belong to you, or if you have just absorbed someone else's emotions. You need to ask yourself if the anxiety or distress is your own or someone else's. Listening to your intuition is the key to determining this. If these emotions do belong to you, you need to investigate them further. Try to figure out the cause, speak to a trusted friend or seek counseling if necessary. If these emotions do not belong to you, you need to figure out who they are coming from. Again, you need to hone in and listen to your intuition.
>
> Once you have been able to do this, you need to find a way to politely remove yourself from the source. Once you are able to get about twenty feet away, take note to see if you start to feel any different. In times like these, we want to be polite and not offend people. It is important to put yourself first. Do not hesitate if you need to change seats. With time, you will develop ways to do this easily.
>
> In order to become aware of what our bodies are telling us, we need to take note in these situations where we feel the discomfort. For most empaths, it is usually their stomachs or gut. For others, it may come in the form of headaches, sore throats, and infections. Empaths need to scan their bodies to see which of their body is their vulnerable point or points. When you notice this symptom, the immediate thing you can do is place our hand on the inflicted area and envision ease and comfort to the area. This technique, when practiced daily,

can strengthen the area. This technique will provide ease and relaxation.

The next thing an empath can do to remove toxic energy is to remember to use their breather. Focus and concentrate on your breath for a few minutes. This will help to center and ground you and reconnect you to your sense of peace.

Quick and fast meditations—which are sometimes referred to as guerilla mediations—can be executed next. This combats negative emotional and physical symptoms very quickly, in fact, in a matter of minutes, a sense of relief can be achieved. These meditations can be done anywhere. These can be done at parties, conferences, work, or even at home. You just need to find a quiet space like a bathroom and meditate there. The first step is to mindfully calm yourself and then focus on love and positivity.

Visualization often helps empaths. The security that comes from it might only be psychological, but it empowers and gives strength to empaths. Your thoughts will actualize. You can envision yourself surrounded by white protective light or a powerful jaguar keeping guard on you. In moments of vulnerability, empaths must use whatever means possible to protect themselves. The spaces between one's vertebrae contribute to reducing pain in one's body. Visualizing pain out of these areas can provide relief. This is done with conscious thought directed to these areas.

Water is a natural cleanser. Taking a bath or shower is very refreshing and soothing. It is a quick and instant way to dissolve stress, anxiety, and accumulated toxins. Take note of how you feel straight after having taken a bath or shower. Not only do they wash away physical dirt and grime but emotional and psychological ones as well.

It is important for an empath to continue to practices the strategies above regularly. This will help you to create a space where you can be nurtured and restored, as well as respond quicker when you are in a negative space. Empaths do not have to take on the world's burdens; they are meant to thrive, flourish, and spread joy and hope in the world. In order to do this, you must take care of and protect yourself first.

Chapter Eight: The Benefits of Meditation

There may not always be ways and means to block or shut out negative energies or emotions, so it helps to arm oneself with some techniques to protect your own energy field. This will help you to be in control of what affects you. The best and most effective way to do this is through meditation.

Finding inner peace and happiness, less anxiety, more positivity, and joy can be found through the ability to control your mind and thoughts. Learning to control the mind is a prerequisite for empaths to have a happy life. The way you feel about something starts with the thoughts you have. To feel happy and connected you need to start with those thoughts. Therefore, thoughts prompt either positive or negative thoughts. Thoughts can keep you from having a good sleep; they take over when you do something menial like driving and can distract you from living fully in the moment. Being able to still the mind is the most empowering thing for an empath. Learning to gain control over your thoughts will take time, but it is well worth the effort. You can do this through meditation. Meditation means that empaths can have better control over thoughts that activate negative emotions. Meditation puts you at a place of equilibrium. When you are able to let go of resistance and anxiety, you make way for inner peace and clarity to enter. Meditations allow you to create the most beneficial starting point for you each day.

Medical Benefits

There are many benefits, besides those specific to empaths that will benefit someone that meditates. Meditation will also improve your immune function and enhance your physical health. Meditation lowers stress levels, anxiety and improves the quality of your breathing. When we learn the benefits of meditation, we will see that it becomes a means to cope with a range of physical disorders and cognitive challenges without the need to take medication. The emotional and health-boosting benefits are based on scientific evidence that can be found everywhere if one bothers to look.

Meditation, when done in the dark, is more beneficial. The darkness helps to keep the pineal gland in good shape, which then positively affects the production of melatonin. Melatonin is produced by the pineal gland when in darkness, is considered the anti-aging hormone that the body produces naturally. So yes, meditation will help in anti-aging, de-stressing, and help you to sleep better. Those who suffer from insomnia or have mild sleeping difficulties are believed to have a melatonin deficiency. Melatonin does not just help to regulate sleep, it is an antioxidant, anti-inflammatory, and prevents and treats many illnesses including cancer. It is well known that the immune system does most of its work at night and that it is believed to be linked to the production of melatonin. We need to spend more time in darkness to produce melatonin. However, modern-day living does not always allow for this. We have street lights and sheer curtains so our bedrooms are letting light in. this reduces the production of melatonin and affects a person's sleep. Meditating before you sleep in complete darkness will aid the production of melatonin. This, together with the ability of meditation to stimulate the pineal gland is proof of the numerous benefits of meditating.

The Basics

Peace of mind and controlling one's thoughts are not just the only benefits to mediation. One has to set time aside every day to practice meditation. It does require commitment and dedication. One should start with a few minutes each day and increase it gradually. People do not have to meditate for hours to reap the benefits. It is important to choose a space where there will be no disturbance. This is trickier to achieve in a household with small children, but with a little negotiation, it can be achieved. To tune out external noise, one can play some gentle, soothing music to meditate to. There is also a myriad of guided meditations that one can purchase and listen to. It is important to have a regular routine before the rewards can be reaped.

Effective Release

Meditation is an exceptionally valuable practice to use to overturn negative thinking that leads to a buildup of stress and anxiety. A quick Google search will lead you to a myriad of studies that show the beneficial effects of meditation. In a 2009 meditation study, researchers at UCLA found that parts of the brain that regulate emotion were considerably larger in long-term practitioners of meditation than those who do not practice meditation. High-resolution magnetic resonance imaging (MRI) was documented that measured the size of areas in the brain such as the hippocampus, the thalamus, and lower temporal gyrus. Researchers noted that people who consistently meditate are able to develop positive emotions, maintain emotional constancy and engage in mindful activities. The participants of this study meditated on average between ten and one and a half hours each day.

Types of Meditation

There are many types of meditation to suit each type of empath. These range from visualization, chanting, breath-work, and trance. Meditation does not have to be indoors. You can meditate while walking by focusing your awareness on the things around you. This could be like the way your feet feel on grass, or how the sunlight feels on your skin. Some of the most common types are outlined below:

Metta Meditation

The goal of this type is to develop an outlook of love and kindness even towards negativity and stress-generating triggers. It is a very useful meditation for empaths who come across energy zappers at work or at family gatherings. During meditation, practitioners send out *loving kindness* to specific people, their families, and friends and to the world in general. With continued regular practice, it will become easier for an empath to incorporate the perspective of *loving kindness* into a habit. An outlook of *loving-kindness* promotes compassion towards oneself and towards others and is especially helpful to remove feelings of anger, frustration, and resentment, while at the same time promoting positive emotions.

Body Scan or Progressive Relaxation

This is a good meditation for empaths trying to learn what their bodies are telling them. It helps empaths to find out where their vulnerable points are, and will help to reduce the effects of negativity and overload in the long term. During this type of meditation, practitioners are required to scan their bodies to identify areas of tension. Once tension is identified, through focus and intention, the tension is released first from one area and then the next. One can start the scan from the feet upwards or from the head down. It is important to give attention to every part of the body. The effects of progressive relaxation encourage relaxation and feelings of peace. It helps empaths to get to a place of equilibrium. It can also be useful to help those who suffer from chronic pain to cope more effectively and to sleep better.

Mindfulness Meditation
One of the most common *mindfulness meditation* prompts meditators to remain present, aware, and in the moment. One has to avoid thinking of the past or future. This is difficult to achieve, but with perseverance comes success. One has to take note of his/her surroundings. This includes noting sights, sounds and smells without attaching any judgment. One of the reasons why mindfulness is so popular is that it can be practiced anywhere and at any time: in the queue at the bank, in the garden, on a walk, and while waiting for the kettle to boil. This type of meditation is useful to empaths because it is so versatile. More scientific research has been invested in the benefits of *mindfulness meditation* because it is so widely practiced. The benefits include reducing the impact of negative thoughts, improving focus and concentration, and reducing emotional reactions to people and situations. All the things an empath needs to conquer.

Breath Awareness Meditation
This is a subcategory of the mindfulness meditation practice that focuses on conscious breathing. Meditators can either count deep and slow breaths, or they just pay attention to the inhale and exhale of each breath. All other thoughts are quieted by ignoring it or telling the brain to refocus. This type of meditation is particularly useful for reducing anxiety and is therefore beneficial to empaths. It is also a meditation that can be practiced anywhere making it useful when one notices a trigger is activated.

Kundalini Yoga
Kundalini yoga is a form of meditation that harmoniously combines movement with incantations and deep breathing. Practitioners usually attend a class led by a teacher. The other popular option is to follow a video or DVD. The benefits include enhanced physical strength and improved positive mental health. These are aspects that empaths need to strengthen and add to their arsenal of protection.

Zen Meditation
A Zen meditation, or Zazen as it is also referred to, is a type of meditation that belongs to the Buddhist practice. Like Kundalini yoga, this practice is composed of specific steps and dedicated postures. Once in a comfortable position, the practitioner pays attention to the breath and observes thought without judging the thinking pattern. If one is struggling with eliminating thoughts, this may be a good meditation to start with. For those empaths that are more physical and need to move, this will also help make the meditation more relaxing.

Transcendental Meditation
For empaths looking for a more devoted spiritual form of meditation, transcendental meditation is a popular option. Meditators are seated comfortably and breathe in and out slowly. Meditators can either concentrate on a mantra that is already determined by a teacher, or of their own choosing such as a positive affirmation. This is a powerful meditation not just to get off toxic and negative energy, but also to strengthen one's empathic abilities.

It is important to find what works for you. It is imperative to be kind, patient, and loving towards yourself rather than criticizing yourself for not doing it right. Self-care and self-love are vital for empaths to thrive. You will know you're on the right track when you begin to feel the amazing benefits that a calm and relaxed mind will bring into your life, and when you can start using your skills to benefit the lives around you.

If meditation is a completely unfamiliar practice to you then here are a few tips to becoming a pro at it.

Tips for Successful Meditation:

Choose a comfortable quiet spot to sit or lie down. There must be nothing that will distract you from your meditated state. All hones should be switched off. The family needs to be told that this is your time and that they cannot disturb you. Using headphones will help to shut out the background noise.

Meditating is better with your eyes closed. If you can't manage this, switch off the lights, or if you're meditating during the day, use eye masks.

Start off slow and easy with just a few minutes and slowly increase the duration as you become proficient at meditation.

Start by counting down from 10 and repeat this until you feel relaxed.

Do not judge yourself or get annoyed if thoughts start to enter your mind. Gently dismiss them and refocus. This may happen many times over so be prepared for that. It is completely natural in the beginning. Everyone experiences this; it will get better with time and practice.

Listening to gentle, soothing music during a meditation helps with focus. One has to pay close attention to the notes of the music. Thoughts will filter in, they are persistent. Without criticism, gently push them aside and remind yourself to refocus.

Another very useful tip often used in meditations is to deliberately place awareness on each part of the body. See and feel light entering the brain and moving down from the head to the face, to the neck and shoulders, and slowly progressing through the body until it reaches the toes. This may not be a timed technique, but it is much easier to focus on and less of a chance of intruding thoughts entering your mind.

If meditation does not quite resonate with you, you can try mindfulness practices that suit your personality and lifestyle:

Mindfulness

This is a practice where you try to remain in the moment and aware of where you are and your experience. One needs an object to anchor their experience. The most common choice is breath, but it could be a sound, a visual or a physical object that helps to encourage mental strength.

Yoga

For those who struggle to sit still and focus, yoga may be the answer. Yoga is the combination of movement with awareness; it reconnects the body, mind, and spirit.

Breathing from the Abdomen

Breathing grounds you and helps to relieve symptoms of stress and anxiety. People mostly take shallow breaths and breathe quite rapidly. One has to learn to slow this process down and breathing from your lungs instead of your chest. As you do this, you will notice that your stomach inflates as you inhale and deflates as you exhale. Initially, one might experience being light-headed, if this happens, stop until you feel normal again before continuing. This type of breathing should be done for a few minutes each to release feelings of tension, stress, and anxiousness.

Breathing from the Nostrils

Another good technique is to breathe from alternate nostrils. It is important to be in a comfortable position, sitting upright, and keeping your eyes closed. The right thumb is positioned on the right nostril, and the right ring finger will linger over the left nostril. When the right nostril is closed, one needs to inhale through the left for three seconds. Thereafter, close the left nostril and breathe through the right nostril for three seconds. This process needs to be repeated for about twenty times. Do not be alarmed if initially, you feel a bit dizzy. If this happens, stop, breathe normally and when it passes, you may resume.

Many people have put off meditation because they believe that it is difficult to achieve. Being still is one thing, but trying to stop one thought from jumping to another is something else. Like all good things in life, it requires effort and won't happen overnight. It may be tricky at first, but it is achievable. Like any other skill, it requires commitment and practice. Start with a few minutes and slowly build up to what suits you. Regularly praising this will build your ability to meditate with ease. Once you have achieved the ability to meditate successfully and start to reap the rewards, there is no turning back. Not only will you achieve clearer insight, but you will deal with stressful situations better.

Quieting the mind is a skill that requires keeping thoughts out of your awareness and focus. Empaths new to meditation and who struggle initially should realize that it will often fail in early attempts, but they should not give up in frustration. As a beginner, one needs to acknowledge that one may not be able to calm one's mind for twenty minutes on a first try. It may take weeks, months or even longer to be successful at this. Empaths have to train their brains to do what it has never done before, that is to keep thoughts and feelings out. No matter how frustrating the first day is, remain committed to a few minutes every day. The strength and relief that empaths can achieve from this technique are bountiful. It is a method that will continue to reward you in many ways.

Chapter Nine: How Empaths Have Helped the World

Empaths have succeeded and made an impact on today's world by embracing their unique qualities. Their ability to identify and step into another person's shoes has allowed empaths all over the world, and through the course of history, to make a social impact and inspire others.

Empaths in Politics

Barack Obama has made numerous speeches referencing the "*empathy deficit*" as modern day society's biggest issue. He believes that by developing a culture of empathy, we can solve many of the issues we face today across the world. He preaches understanding and empathy rather than hatred and division. One of his famous quotes is: *"Learning to stand in somebody else's shoes, to see through their eyes, that's how peace begins. And it's up to you to make that happen."*

Way back in 1971, C.P. Ellis, demonstrated his empathic ability. He found himself at a top position in the Ku Klux Klan. He initially joined, following in the footsteps of his father, because he believed that all black people were the cause of the poverty his family was facing. He was part of a community forum to solve racial tensions in schools. He headed this forum with a woman he hated. She was a black activist named Ann Atwater. However, this provided a platform for him to identify with her needs and realized that they were fighting the same cause and he was blaming black people instead of the real culprits who were white capitalists and politicians. He later became a civil rights campaigner and he and Ann remained friends. He publicly denounced his Ku Klux Klan membership and was able to take responsibility for his choices by fighting for rights of all people including black people in America through his ability to empathize.

We cannot mention politics and empaths by mentioning the famous Mahatma Gandhi. In his crusade for Indian independence from British rule, he decided to undergo an empathic immersion. He believed that he could not truly fight for the rights of people until he fully understood them. He substituted his barrister's suit for a loincloth. He lived the life of the peasant farmers of India from 1917 to 1930. He embraced all aspects of their lives even the jobs that were considered 'untouchable' to many, like cleaning latrines. He penetrated deep racial divides in India and uttered words which are still relevant today: *"I am a Muslim! And a Hindu and a Christian and a Jew—and so are all of you."* This is a statement that embodies all that it is to be an empath.

Empathic Actors

Effective actors need to fully embrace the roles they undertake. For this, they have to find ways to deeply identify and understand their characters. Many dedicated actors have undergone empathy immersion in order to fully understand the characters they intend to play. Hillary Swank won an Oscar for her role as a transgendered man, Brandon Teena. His male friends raped and him when they discovered that he had female genitalia. Hillary Swank also undertook an empathy immersion for the preparation of this role by cutting off her hair and dressing in her husband's clothes for a month. In this way, she identified with people with a sexual identity crisis and the harassment they face. Through her role, she raised awareness and tried to bring about understanding and empathy for gay, lesbian, and transgender people.

Charlize Theron gained weight for her roles as an overworked mother of three children and her role as a serial killer. She did this so that she could fully feel what life was like for these characters. This ability to embrace an immersive empathy makes her successful at acting and raises empathy in the audience.

Empathy Through Authors

George Orwell immersed himself into an empathic experience to discover what life was really like for every day working class people. He lived as a beggar on the streets of London as a means to understand oppressed people. He raised awareness through his book 'Down and Out in Paris and London' and continued to highlight marginalized communities.

Harriet Beecher Stowe fought against slavery in 1852 through her book titled 'Uncle Tom's Cabin'. She highlighted the horrors that slaves went through, which eventually led to rebellions and the American Civil War.

Social Activists

In 1206, Giovanni Bernadone, better known as *St. Francis of Assisi* identified with the poor by being a beggar for a day. This experience led him to serve the poor and lepers in Rome.

Many years later, in 1959, a white Texas-born man decided to see what life was like as a black individual living in America by dyeing his skin black. He wrote a book to describe his experiences called 'Black Like Me'. He outlined in his book how people need to use empathy to change their biases and stereotypes and treat people better. His message in his book states: *"If only we could put ourselves in the shoes of others to see how we would react, then we might become aware of the injustices of discrimination and the tragic inhumanity of every kind of prejudice."*

Conclusion

We hope that in reading this book you have gained insight and understanding of what it is to be an empath. We hope that this understanding brings peace, acceptance, and clarity into your life. We hope that the tools, techniques, and ways provided will help empaths cope with the world. It may be a difficult journey of discovery for an empath, but there will be much to be grateful for. Using the strengths of an empath like intuition, compassion, depth, and a connection to people and the surrounding gives an empath the capacity to help others. In a world that lacks compassion and kindness, empaths are more needed than ever. Empaths from all over the world and across different eras have helped to champion social justice, causes, or raise awareness of the plight of others in some way. Empowered empaths are what the world needs now.

There is much for an empath to be grateful for. Empaths can experience the greatest joys and passion, are synchronized to the beauty and energy of the world, can show compassion, awareness, and great depth. These gifts must shine into the world, enlightening it and bringing healing for everyone. For this to happen, empaths must listen to their intuition, instincts, and feelings. They must strengthen their ability to remain centered when surrounded by chaos and negativity. Empaths must embrace who they are and accept their sensitivities. When this happens, they can enhance the lives of the people around them. When empaths do not learn how to cope with and recognize the feeling of being overwhelmed or being stressed, it can lead to depression, panic attacks, addiction, food, medication, and isolation.

The strategies of setting boundaries, time limits, and shielding techniques can help empaths navigate a sea of negative energies. Together with meditation, time apart, and being in nature, empaths can empower themselves and remain centered and grounded majority of the time. These are all strategies that can be learned and mastered with practice.

When empaths are surrounded by love and peace, they will blossom and offer the world many gifts. When they are surrounded by negativity, pain, and loss, they will absorb all these emotions and result in feeling exhausted, overwhelmed, and drained. An empath's sensitivity can lead them to shy away from intimate relationships, but empaths can enjoy the comforts and joys of intimacy and cohabitation. By regularly practicing the techniques in this book, empaths will be armed with survival and coping strategies with which to negotiate the modern world. Empaths can feel and be open instead of choosing isolation and numbness. Empaths can surrender and feel instead of constantly blocking. With the acceptance and understanding of what it is to be an empath, empaths can communicate and educate family and friends, thereby, fostering a deeper understanding and connection between them. When supported by people who appreciate and honor an empath's abilities, empaths can grow and blossom. The purpose of empaths is to use their sensitivities and compassion to show and create love in the world.

Enneagram:

The Only Book You Will Ever Need to Build Strength for Your Life. Discover The 9 Personalities Types. Evolve Your Personality and Become Self Aware!

Table of Contents

Introduction..75
Chapter 1: The Enneagram and the Self................................76
Chapter 2: The History of the Enneagram.............................81
Chapter 3: The Structure of the Enneagram.........................83
Chapter 4: The 9 Personality Types.......................................86
Chapter 5: The Wings..117
Chapter 6: Health of the Self..120
Chapter 7: Personality Test..126
Conclusion...140

© Copyright 2018 by Ian Baron - All rights reserved.

The follow eBook is reproduced below with the goal of providing information that is as accurate and reliable as possible. Regardless, purchasing this eBook can be seen as consent to the fact that both the publisher and the author of this book are in no way experts on the topics discussed within and that any recommendations or suggestions that are made herein are for entertainment purposes only. Professionals should be consulted as needed prior to undertaking any of the action endorsed herein.

This declaration is deemed fair and valid by both the American Bar Association and the Committee of Publishers Association and is legally binding throughout the United States.

Furthermore, the transmission, duplication or reproduction of any of the following work including specific information will be considered an illegal act irrespective of if it is done electronically or in print. This extends to creating a secondary or tertiary copy of the work or a recorded copy and is only allowed with express written consent from the Publisher. All additional right reserved.

The information in the following pages is broadly considered to be a truthful and accurate account of facts and as such any inattention, use or misuse of the information in question by the reader will render any resulting actions solely under their purview. There are no scenarios in which the publisher or the original author of this work can be in any fashion deemed liable for any hardship or damages that may befall them after undertaking information described herein.

Additionally, the information in the following pages is intended only for informational purposes and should thus be thought of as universal. As befitting its nature, it is presented without assurance regarding its prolonged validity or interim quality. Trademarks that are mentioned are done without written consent and can in no way be considered an endorsement from the trademark holder.

Introduction

Congratulations on downloading *Enneagram* and thank you for doing so.

The following chapters will discuss several different aspects of what constitutes the Enneagram. Since the 1980's, the Enneagram has been used to evaluate someone's personality and reveal the true self. Its true origin reaches much further back beyond that, and as time has passed, the Enneagram has had many different people try to alter its interpretation. This has created some confusion. This book aims to clear up the mystifications that have been surrounding the Enneagram for far too long.

There are several different aspects to the Enneagram that are often overlooked. The Wings and integration/disintegration points are only some of the very important pieces of the Enneagram that do not get covered often. Without being familiar with the entire Enneagram, there will always be confusion surrounding it. In this book, just about every single piece of the Enneagram will be covered. From the 9 different types of dominant personalities, all the way down to how they interact with each other, the mysteries of the Enneagram will be unveiled to you. There will also be a personality test to help you along the path of self-discovery. If you have been wondering who you are, who you *really* are, then the Enneagram is here to help answer that question.

There are plenty of books on this subject on the market, thanks again for choosing this one! Every effort was made to ensure it is full of as much useful information as possible, please enjoy!

Chapter 1: The Enneagram and the Self

Do you know yourself? Are you sure? Can you really explain the reasons for every action you have ever performed? Do you really know the root causes that underline every emotion you have ever felt? Are you capable of understanding the inspiration that has preceded every thought that has ever formulated inside your mind? Unless you have already braved the opaque waters of self-reflection, the answers to these questions should be a strong and resounding NO!

Since the birth of humanity, most people have simply acted or reacted, without delving into the motivations that dictate their actions. This is because we are human beings, far from perfect but high above all the other creatures that we share the planet earth with. Since humans are the highest and most complex out of all the intelligence on earth, it comes with the territory that our thoughts, emotions, and actions are infinitely more complicated than every other living creature. This, upon the first realization, can seem like a bad luck of the draw or being dealt an unfair card from the deck of life. Just by being born as humans, we are confounded into an existence that is more confusing and complicated to navigate through than every other creature on earth.

Compare the life of a human to the life of a deer. A deer, lower in the scale of mental/emotional development and somatic functions than a person, does not have anywhere near the amount of variability to sift through as does a human being. When a deer is scared, it runs away. When it is hungry or thirsty, it fills its stomach. During mating season, it looks for a mate. When it is tired, it sleeps. When it has found its herd, it romps and travels with them. Instinct pervades every decision a deer makes and gives it an existence that is closer to automatic than cognitive. This – comparing a deer to a human – may seem course, because it is. Among creatures lower in scale than humans, there certainly is variability in what they do and in the types of personalities they display, but even so, they still do not have to ponder the great questions that many of us ask ourselves all too often; "Who am I?" "Why did I do that?" "What was I thinking at that moment?"

Animals, insects, plants, and microbes do not have to waddle through the muddy waters of self-discovery. Their existences are simple, automatic, and one could even argue, destined to fate. Even if a creature lower than a human was to act out of character, they would not question why they did so. Nor can they even conceptualize the idea of self-improvement and prevent their negative traits from manifesting again. They simply live to live until they die and then nature creates another one to fill in the gap that they have left behind after expiring. That may sound harsh, but self-discovery is concerned with the truth, and the truth can hurt equally as much as it can heal.

On the other hand, humans are constantly berated with new experiences, environments, and stimuli. Compared to a deer, our lives are far from simple and automatic – or at least they should be. Every single day we have to make judgment calls and perform actions that can have consequences that extend far past the current moment. This applies to even the most common and mundane of our activities. Like a deer, we get hungry and sleepy, but we can decide what to eat and how much of it. We can decide when to go to sleep and set alarms to tell us that it's time to wake up. We can even bypass meals and sleep or change our diets along with sleeping arrangements. These examples of hunger and sleep are extremely baseline. Now, just push the idea a little further. Remember back to a recent business meeting, social gathering or a date that you went on. How many thoughts did you have during those interactions? How many different feelings passed through you? What actions did you perform, or choose not to perform? Surely you encountered a wider range of sensations than a deer does in its daily life. Upon the first realization of the consequences that are attached to our natural mental/emotional superiority over lower lifeforms, it really can seem like us humans have drawn the short end of the stick. We are forced to decipher more options and overcome more challenges than everything else.

We have to manage a wider range of cognitive functions, both positive and negative, than all the other beasts of the world.

Without question, humans have the most complicated lives on the planet. However, we have something to compensate for this seemingly apparent disadvantage. Human beings can self-reflect. Unlike an animal, we can probe into our psyches and better learn who we really are, and thus, understand why we do the things we do, feel the things we feel, and think the thoughts we think. We can use our powers of associative learning and self-discipline to better understand our own motivations and behavioral patterns. We can do what an animal cannot, which is learning about ourselves. After that, we can begin to (through hard work and allotting time) start to enhance which aspects of ourselves that we find beneficial and remove the aspects that stunt us from reaching a higher potential. We have not drawn the shorter stick in nature; it only appears that way at first glance.

Even so, to fully utilize our latent abilities and direct how our individual growth develops, we require tools (another advantage we have over other creatures). Among the many different cognitive tools that exist there is one known as the Enneagram which has been designed to do directly aid in the process of self-reflection.

Consider the Enneagram to be a simplified schematic of the human psyche. Now, keep in mind that even though the Enneagram may be simplified, the human psyche is the most complicated concept that we know of. Modern science still struggles to define what consciousness actually is and what it is not. In many ways, the questions of "Who am I" or "Why did I do that?" are the forerunners to the bigger mysteries of existence. Figuring out the answers to those questions is the first step to understanding your own consciousness, and thus, understanding who you really are. The Enneagram can be used as a sort of roadmap to help clear the road of your consciousness and show the way to who you really are, instead of wandering through life like a clueless animal that is completely at the mercy of its environment.

To understand the Enneagram is not the easiest task upon first discovery but, with time and practice, it will help clear the waters of confusion that surround yourself and others around you. The more you learn about it, the clearer its implications will become and help to shed light on the questions of why you, or someone else, may think or act in a certain way.

The Enneagram can be broken-down into one little symbol. It consists of the numbers 1-9 and intersecting lines between each number. When someone first sees the Enneagram, they may write it off as just some confusing chart, a mess that lacks cohesion. This is the first error that many people make when first trying to swim across the channel from ignorance to self-discovery. Every number and line encased within the Enneagram contains a wealth of specifics meanings. Nothing in the image is arbitrary or random. It just has to be learned how to be read, then it can be studied, and then you can use the emblem of the Enneagram to discover who you really are, as well as see the truths of other people. The Enneagram will unbiasedly reveal your own strengths, virtues, limitations, and vices. The Enneagram will tell you what you need to improve about yourself. It will help you to discover which traits of the self should be removed if you desire to grow into a more efficient version of who you already are. It will aid you in the process of no longer living like an automatic animal and graduating into a completely self-sufficient human being. It will give you the set of keys that can unlock the doors to your life that have always been shut tight. It will help you to truly know yourself on every level.

The first thing most people will notice when seeing the Enneagram are the numbers 1-9. These 9 numbers are all representative of the different types of personality a person can have. Each one of these personality types should not be summed up into only one or two sentences. Yes, that can be done, and in many different mediums related to the Enneagram, it has been. Yet, the enneagram is used to learn everything you can about your own personality. Not superficially, but in depth. Remember that the enneagram is a schematic of the human psyche and that humans have the most complex psyches on the planet. One-word descriptions for something so complicated lacks both scope and substance.

To fully understand the Enneagram, and understand everything about you, every point of interest involved in the symbol must be taken into consideration. The major points of interest when studying the enneagram are:

- The 9 different personality types.
- The wings (secondary personality traits).
- The 9 levels of development of the personality.
- Integration and disintegration points.

Every piece of the Enneagram will be covered in this book – every number, line, shape, and all the points of interest listed above. But before delving into all of that, it would be wise to learn a little bit of the history that helped construct the enneagram. You are welcome to skip ahead and go straight to studying the enneagram if you wish but doing so is not recommended. Consider the history of the Enneagram a primer for what is to come. Many people have begun their research into the Enneagram expecting a short and insightful cognitive spell only to realize that it is a symbol that can be studied for an entire lifetime, and even then, there is still more to learn about it. You are never done discovering who you really are. You do have to start somewhere though, and the Enneagram is one of the best places to begin your journey of self-discovery.

Chapter 2: The History of the Enneagram

Covering every aspect of what has developed the Enneagram of personality would consist of not only just one book but an entire chronicling of all human thought. That may sound like a lofty statement, but it surely is not. The origin of the Enneagram can be traced back to the days of antiquity. In truth, it is an expansion of spiritual and early psychological concepts that have been streamlined to be understood by a larger and more contemporary audience. Esoteric concepts such as the "Law of Three" or "Law of Seven" are concluded in some circles to be directly connected to the development of the Enneagram. The work of Eliphas Levi, Helena Blavatsky, Pythagoras, among many others who are renown in the realm of esoteric workings, have all been attributed to having at least some input with constructing the modern-day version of the Enneagram (or using their own versions of the symbol). It is recommended to, eventually, study some of the theories that the previously named people developed, but that is for a later time along with your journey of self-exploration.

The currently used model of the Enneagram is accredited to being discovered (or altered) by Oscar Ichazo. He was not the first person to show the Enneagram to the world at large, but he was the one who attributed the 9 basic personality types to the image, which is what the Enneagram is most famously known for in our current era. Oscar Ichazo was the man who took the Enneagram of antiquity and shaped it into the Enneagram of personality, as it is known today. Even though the Enneagram has origins that trace back much further, Ichazo's interpretation of the symbol only goes back to the 1960's.

Oscar Ichazo was a very well learned man who traveled abroad. He was born in Bolivia, moved to Peru, and then relocated to Argentina. Later in life, he traveled to different parts of South America and Asia where he learned a large variety of different spiritual and psychological theories and techniques. This all led up to him establishing the Arica school in Chile. At this school, he focused his teachings on understanding and expanding the human consciousness. It was believed back in the era of antiquity, and still by many people today that grasping the truth of the self and the nature of existence as a whole can only be accurately understood by first understanding your own consciousness. Although Ichazo used many different tools and symbols to explore the human consciousness, the Enneagram of personality (with the 9 basic personality types he attributed to it) became one of the main instruments he often employed.

While Oscar Ichazo was teaching his lessons at the school of Arica, he also taught two American writers and psychologists, John Lilly and Claudio Naranjo. Claudio Naranjo, later on, began spreading his own particular interpretations of the Enneagram in America during the 1970s. Since then, many other authors, psychologists, and spiritual leaders have spread their own version and lessons of the Enneagram. This has created a double-edged sword of confusion and debate to its practical use and applications. In truth, the Enneagram can be extrapolated to represent many different things, but its focus has always been concentrated on development and understanding of the self.

The theories and uses of the Enneagram differ among those who attest to it, as some attribute it more to the soul while others like to remove spiritual implications from it. Whether your particular journey of self-realization is imbued with spiritual essence, or if you select to omit spirituality from studying the Enneagram, it can be used the same way. Begin learning about it with the mindset that you are most comfortable with. As you learn more about the Enneagram, and yourself, be aware that your goals and current concepts of understanding may change quite drastically.

Chapter 3: The Structure of the Enneagram

Oscar Ichazo specifically used the Enneagram to dissect and explore different aspects of the human soul. He placed a special importance on how the different essences of a person may become distorted or fall into unbeneficial states of ego. Drawing inspiration from many different schools of spiritual and psychological thought, including the Tree of Life, Ichazo established a wide variety of correspondences to each of the 9 dominant personality types. These included:

- The major characteristic of the dominant personality type.
- What the ego could negatively fixate its attention towards, operating within the sphere of a specific personality type.
- A frame of mind associated with a dominant personality type when it was exalted (sometimes called a "Holy Idea").
- Baseline desires and fears that were attached to a dominant personality type. Along with these were also the attributed vices and virtues.
- Certain temptations that were harder for a dominant personality type to resist.
- Integration and disintegration points for each type of personality. These are also known as "growth" and "stress" points. For now, think of these as how someone's personality can alter when they are in good or bad moods.

As more people started adding and subtracting their own correspondences to the Enneagram, much of the spiritual aspects have been lessened. The basic model of the Enneagram has not changed in a long time though, and no matter how you decide to study the symbol, the schematic remains the same. The quickest way to make sense of the Enneagram is to personally draw one. Grab a pen and a piece of paper and follow these directions.

- First, draw a circle. A circle is a symbol of unity, wholeness, and nothing being separate from each other. Consider the circle as a sphere of operation. Whatever exists outside the circle has no effect on what takes place within the circle. Whatever exists within the circle is connected to everything else within the sphere of operation.

- Label the numbers 1-9 around the perimeter of the circle. Start with 9 at the top, then going clockwise, list the numbers 1-8. When you are done, the number 9 should be sandwiched between the number 1 (to its right) and the number 8 (to its left). These numbers are the 9 basic dominant personality types.

- Draw a triangle between the numbers 9, 6, and 3. Consider the triangle to be symbolic of something coming into being, the first possible shape.
- Draw a line connecting to each number in the following order; 1-4-2-8-5-7-1. Drawing a connecting line to these numbers will create an irregular hexagram. Think of the irregular hexagram as a representation of abstraction being brought into form.

- Outside of the circle, write the following words next to each number. 9 – Mediator. 1 – Perfectionist. 2 – Helper. 3 – Achiever. 4 – Individualist. 5 – Investigator. 6 – Loyalist. 7 – Enthusiast. 8 – Challenger.

Congratulations! You have just drawn the Enneagram of personality. Between the images used in this book and the picture you have just drawn, you can begin to use the Enneagram to explore yourself. These few building blocks of a circle, triangle, irregular hexagram, intersecting lines, and the numbers 1-9 may not seem like much at first, but when you learn what they all mean, illumination will begin to be unfurled to you.

The words you wrote next to the numbers 1-9 are the names of the different dominant personality types. According to different sources, some of these personality types have different names. Do not get stuck on the minute details of the Enneagram and remember that one-word descriptions of the 9 different dominant personality types are only a starting point - not the finish line of understanding. As you discover more about it and become capable of drawing your own conclusions, you may alter names and associations as you see fit.

Now that you have been introduced to the Enneagram and know some of the histories that have helped develop it, you can safely begin to study each personality type individually and begin to discover the aspects of yourself that you didn't know about before.

Chapter 4: The 9 Personality Types

To fully understand everything that makes up someone's personality, the entire sphere of the Enneagram must be taken into consideration. The 9 basic personality types are only the start of studying the Enneagram and yourself. It should always be remembered though that every person has a dominant personality – which will be one of the basic 9 types listed in this chapter. It should also be made clear that your dominant personality will not always be acting with precedence over other aspects of your personality. Your secondary traits, as well as other factors, will have an effect on how you are thinking or behaving at any given moment. In truth, every person has all of the basic 9 personality types inside their psychosis. However, no matter what stimulus alters our personality temporarily, you will always return to your basic personality type. This is why the basic personality types are labeled as the *Dominant Personality*. Before diving into the secondary personality traits, as well as all the other extrapolated pieces of the human personality, it's best to learn what the 9 dominant personality types are. We start at the top and work our way down the tree of the Enneagram.

Although behavioral science is still developing, it is understood that we develop a dominant personality early in life. Hereditary factors, family traditions, environment, social, and early childhood experiences all come together to create a dominant personality that we clothe ourselves in. Think of your dominant personality as a persona that you wear to navigate and understand the world around you. It can change, for better or worse, as time goes by, but no matter how your personality alters, it will always have roots stemming from the dominant personality that you developed during the first four or five years of your life. You are the soil. The dominant personality is the first root to spring from the soil, and everything else that develops after are the fruit that hangs from the tree of your personality. The tree of your personality can either thrive with time or wither. Using a tool like the Enneagram will help you to make it thrive.

Along with describing what each of the 9 dominant personality types is, there will be a list of the metadata that goes along with each one. These will include the virtues, vices, desires, fears, what the ego can fixate on, exalted ideals, temptations, and integration and disintegration points. The integration and disintegration points will be explained more in detail later, but a cursory explanation should be given here.

When someone, let's use a person with a type 1 dominant personality as an example, is having a bad week, they will not act like themselves, so to speak. They will move away from the normal dominant personality and "fall" into a different type of person. This is known as disintegrating. When a person with a type 1 dominant personality "falls" into a slump, they will disintegrate into a type 4. Whenever they pull out of this slump and return to their normal selves, they will readopt the persona of a type 1. On the other end of the spectrum, when they are having a good week, they will integrate into a Type 7. Then when their good luck streak winds down, they will return to Type 1. Be aware at all times that there is no superiority in relation to the numbers assigned to each type of personality. Just because someone is a 1 or a 4 does not mean they are better off than someone with a different number. The numbers are used for organizational purposes only. Later on, when the integration/disintegration points are covered in more detail, this will all become clearer. For now, just be aware that when someone is in a slump or on a winning streak, their personality will change temporarily.

It should also be understood that none of the 9 basic personality types are exclusive to either gender. Although they may be expressed in different manners, both men and women have all of the basic 9 personality types within their psyches. Your gender will only affect the way that your dominant personality presents itself, not what your dominant personality actually is. Also, remember that any of these 9 dominant personality types can all manifest in different ways and that each one is working in tandem with secondary personality traits as well as other factors incorporated in the human psyche. In other words, although your dominant personality type may be a 3, on some days, you may act more like a 4 or 7. Recognizing these sorts of fluctuations in your behavioral pattern is just another part along the road to self-discovery.

Type 1: The Perfectionist and Reformer

Type 1 people are the kind of people that feel they must be correct with everything they do. They believe themselves to adhere to a higher moral code than other people. They place strong values on being recognized for their integrity and having a higher standard of principles. They are typically very disciplined people and are not the easiest to sway away from their goals. Structure and order are important concepts to Type 1s as they tend to want the world around them to be as disciplined as they are. Type 1s are the kind of people that you can rely on to uphold the rules and follow procedures down to the letter. These are the kind of people that you can trust to get a job done well the first time you ask, and they can probably do it without asking for help. Most Type 1s do not only mind hard work but thrive while doing it. However, if their work environment is not as perfect as they are, then they may have trouble trying to complete a task. Due to this, some Type 1s can be slow to move from the planning stage into action. They can be procrastinators, or not even begin some projects at all if they don't see the immediate value in doing so. They can be somewhat slow at times to make decisions while they meticulously comb through all the variables of every decision they make.

Type 1s make good leaders, although those they are leading may think they are too strict or rigid. They are also very talented at noticing all the finer details and catching the little things that others would often miss. They can organize and turn a wild incoherent mess into something where all the pieces fit together. They can shape chaos into order.

Due to their need to feel perfect, they can be susceptible to harsh judgment towards themselves and others. When a Type 1 discovers that they have made a mistake, they take it more harshly than others would. They can also hold every single little thing, including other people, up to their standards – which can come across as very unfair and unrealistic. They can be prone to self-doubt and question every action they make. A common Type 1 will often ask themselves if they are good enough to accomplish whatever they are trying to do and often second guess things that they had already done.

Type 1s do not have much patience towards the irresponsible. They are prone to bursts of anger but often will try to hide it from others. Being angry can be a sign of not being perfect, which is all they aspire to be. When trying to hide their anger, they may display subtle body language to reflect their anger or just go as silent as a stone. They may even start to become extremely formal and overtly polite as a way of masking the imperfection of anger. If they do become angry enough to seek some sort of vengeance, they will most likely extract it with a cold and calculating methodology. They like to plan ahead, and even their schemes of revenge must be executed perfectly. An easy way to get on the bad side of a Type 1 and arouse their anger is to point out their imperfections and be as critical of them as they are of others. A Type 1 is already judging themselves on a regular basis, and when someone else starts doing it to them as well, they simply don't want to hear it, especially since the person who is criticizing them is already imperfect in their eyes.

Type 1s can be hard to argue with. They already believe themselves to be correct and may completely detach themselves from the present moment. Or they may get all too caught up in it. It depends on if they think the other people around them are worthy of bothering over.

Type 1s are also the reformers. They fix errors and strive to set everything in its proper place. Spiritually speaking, they seek the highest platitude. They will endure whatever challenge they must so they can learn, grow, and ascend onto higher plains. There can even be a sacrificial aspect to Type 1s. If they understand that there is something they must do, or stop doing, to achieve a higher grade of consciousness, then a Type 1 will readily meet the challenge head-on. Type 1s can become dogmatic and may misinterpret or discard concepts that do not fit into their dogma. It can take a lot of time for them to learn their lessons. Yet, when they do learn them, they go straight to work trying to reform their errors.

Type 1 at a glance

- **Virtue:** Being serene. Feeling as if there are no other improvements needed.
- **Vice:** Prone to anger when feeling that everything is not as it should be.
- **Common Temptation:** Criticizing others and themselves.
- **Common Desire:** Being recognized as being correct. Being in balance.
- **Common Fear:** Being wrong or swayed by other people. Being out of balance.
- **Exalted Ideals:** Being correct in their principles. Serving a worthy purpose. Correcting errors of the self and their environment.
- **Egoic Challenge:** Type 1s have to try very hard not to hold resentment against everything that does not fall in line with what they consider to be perfection. They need to let go of the desire to judge and control everything around them.
- **Integration Point:** 7.
- **Disintegration Point:** 4

Type 2: The Helper and Giver

Type 2s aim to develop strong relationships with others. They will often go out of their way to win over another person. These types of people are the helping hands, the people you can call upon when stuck in a jam. They feel a sense of satisfaction when they know they have helped someone. Generally, they also like to receive recognition for their efforts and are more likely to assist someone they know who can spread a good word of their reputation, but they may also feel a sudden impulse to help out a stranger as well. The major motivation behind their actions is a longing to feel apricated, even needed, by other people. This is not vanity, as Type 2s are also humble people. A type 2 depends upon the opinions of others to give value to themselves. This can parlay into random acts of kindness and generosity. They can also influence others with their kindness and spread it around infectiously. To a Type 2, doing so is a roundabout way of making the world a better place to live.

Every type of dominant personality has positive and negative traits. Type 2s sound almost perfect, but it should be known that they can lack confidence if they are not receiving praise from others. They don't just want to help; they need to help someone to feel as if they are worthy human beings. Type 2s want people to depend on them. There could be a deeper confliction hidden here, as if a Type 2 may not feel that they deserve love or affection for who they are and must earn it by helping other people. Some Type 2s can come across as manipulative. They help someone fully expecting the help to be returned to them and are not offering assistance for free even if they pretend they are. They will often give out many compliments but expect other people to do the same to them.

Type 2s are crowd-pleasers. They are the sort of people who will show up to a party with gifts or buy everyone at the bar an extra round. Most people are attracted to them since they can come off as warm and comforting. They don't mind giving up some of their time or resources if it means that other people will recognize them for their efforts. A Type 2 may not ask for anything in return for all that they give – but they still expect their good deeds to be rewarded in one manner or another.

Type 2s can be empathetic. They can notice when someone else is having a problem and will leap right into action to fix whatever is wrong. Because of their giving nature, they can become offended when ignored or their efforts are not recognized. They detest being taken advantage of, but still may let it happen anyway.

All the giving and helping that a Type 2 does is really a tactic to establish good relationships with people. Deep relationships are extremely important to them. Their generosity is on open display and acts like a net to catch the attention and goodwill of others. They also try to resist negative stimulus and want everyone else around them to act as generous as they do. They can give advice without even being asked and are very quick to defend someone that they think has been wronged.

Since Type 2s are empaths, they can notice problems and desires that other people don't even notice about themselves. This can backfire on them though as they can spend too much time and effort on others and not themselves. They can also be susceptible to inflated egos if they are praised too much, and most of their social circle depends upon them to help all the time. Still, they are naturally humble people and have their boosted egos deflated if they fail to correctly help someone. They can also worry about other people when it is not necessary. One of the more detrimental things about a Type 2 is that they may lack the ability to do things alone. They need someone else to tell them that they did well. They can also become attention seekers.

They can become so wrapped up in other people that they can miss many things about themselves. They often don't realize that the reason they are helping others is due to wanting something in return for all the assistance they give. They can also force themselves onto people, and then lose interest in them quite quickly. Conflicts of interest may arise in their lives if they are trying to help more than one person and have to pick and choose who deserves it more. This can also scatter their focus and use of energy and fail to recognize that different people have different needs and desires, or attitudes and values. A Type 2 may try to help someone who doesn't need it and just get in the way. Or they may assume what someone's values are and become crushed when they learn that the person they are trying to help does not view the world the same way they do. Since they desire intimacy and deep connections so much, other people may just think of them as clingy.

They can subconsciously express their own needs onto others without realizing it. This indirect way of communicating can create rifts and delays in achieving their goals. They can also make the mistake of thinking everyone else is in need, even if the people they are trying to help are doing just fine. They can mistake this as being taken for granted. A Type 2 may dislike someone, but still jump in to help them anyway since they think that will increase the bond. They can brag about how helpful they are and have a fear of being rejected. They really just want to be loved and are doing everything they can to attract love towards them.

When Type 2ss are in their highest aspect, they won't expect anything in return. They give just to give and giving is its own reward. An exalted Type 2 will keep a positive mindset and believe that, even if they are not around to help, someone else will step in and fill their role. They will also understand that to better help others, they must be able to take care of themselves first. They understand that along with spreading love around, self-love is equally as important.

Spiritually, there is a sense of sacrifice here as well, but not the same that is associated with Type 1s. A Type 1 will sacrifice what they need to so they can become better for themselves, to raise their consciousness to higher planes. A Type 2 will sacrifice for the good of others and try to lift other people up to higher spiritual arenas with them.

Type 2 at a glance

- **Virtue:** Being Humble. They are prone to humility and can induce it without much effort.
- **Vice:** Too much pride. They can fall into a belief that they are the source of another person's happiness.
- **Common Temptation:** Manipulating other people with their kindness, including themselves and ignoring their own needs.
- **Common Desire:** Love.
- **Common Fear:** Not being loved, despite all they do.
- **Exalted Ideals:** Being free. If everyone is helping out each other, then there should be no more hurdles left to overcome.
- **Egoic Challenge:** Extreme flattery. They can become fixated on wanting other people to tell them how great they are.
- **Integration Point:** 4
- **Disintegration Point:** 8

Type 3: The Achiever and Performer

Type 3s are very concerned with image. They prefer to have the world around them notice that they are the very best at whatever they set themselves to. They often excel in whatever field of work they decide to enter. They are adaptable and efficient. These are some of the hardest working people out there and are often recognized as being pillars of the workplace. Types 3s often reached their goals and do so with gusto. Type 3s on the higher end of the spectrum serves as an inspiration to others. On the lower end, they can be dismissive and selfish. Type 3s place a larger emphasis on what they are doing, not on who they are outside of trying to reach their goals. Almost everything involved in the life of a Type 3 revolves around the idea of winning and losing.

They have a high drive for success and are very ambitious. Nothing matters as much to a Type 3 as results. How they get the results is another matter. Expect high levels of energy to surround type 3s as they are go-getters. They can alter their persona to match whatever task needs to be completed. They are capable of altering many different aspects of themselves. They can wear different guises and impress a large array of people. Some of them are not above lying or bending the rules a bit to stack things in their favor. Still, other Type 3s hold honesty as a high esteem and will place the concept on a pedestal.

They can be fiercely competitive even when there is no worthwhile reward to gain for their efforts. This can turn away many of the people they are trying to impress. They often seek out forms of competition even in their recreational activities, alone or on a team. They are also selective about whom they socialize with. They like to be on the winning team. This can make them good leaders, if even for the wrong reasons.

When a 3 makes a mistake, they are more likely to look at it as a learning experience than a failure. They can be closed minded though and overlook something that they don't understand - thinking that it is not worth their precious time. They think fast on their feet, and this can sometimes lead them to miss the little things, never stopping to smell the roses or appreciate someone else's good values. Also, when a 3 does not have a goal to reach, they can become wayward and start attaching value to missions that are not important. They can make a mountain out of an anthill. They can suffer from confusion of identity since they place so much value on work and accomplishments. They think they are their job, instead of realizing that their job is just an extension of who they really are. Type 3s can also misunderstand that their constant drive for winning is actually born of the need to compare themselves to other people. Type 3s can be thrown off-kilter when discovering that someone else may not care about all their worldly accomplishments. They can become self-conscious, and not in a good way.

They are capable of separating their emotions from their actions since emotions can get in the way of winning. They are not the best when it comes to deeper genuflection. They can also pretend to ignore feelings of despair and anxiety, even if these are traits that they should work through to become more successful. By ignoring sadness, they instead exude negativity in the form of anger. They also waver in front of authority and can become brown noses or try far too hard to impress someone up to the point where they come across as a nuisance. They do not take many risks, preferring to stay on the side of safety and success.

Despite the drive of a Type 3, their self-conscious nature places the most value on how other people perceive them. They are aiming for success not so much to better themselves, but to impress other people. Externally, they are very optimistic, but there is a strong fear of failure boiling inside their hearts. Masking their true feeling and fears can eventually create a web of stress that can plague their minds and distract them from truly opening up. Short outbursts and change of character are not uncommon in them. They may be winners, but unless someone else is announcing their victories, they will feel like losers.

When a 3 is discovered lying or not being who they really are, they can become defensive and spiteful. They may also spend too much time trying to impress the wrong people when what they should be doing is calming down and smelling the roses. Their confusions of identity are often noticed by other people before they notice it themselves. They are very good at doing what they set their minds to and adapting, but not so good at entering unfamiliar territory where the advantage is not stacked in their favor. They can also become delusional when they start to believe their own hype too much.

They can be emotionally closed off and are not willing to sustain a difficult heart to heart conversation. This can make their romantic lives a blithering mess. Often, a Type 3 will want a partner that is subservient to their aspirations. They also may not take criticism very well and can be labeled as coldhearted, even if it is not true. They may blame other people for making them look bad even if it is their own fault and can be very impatient. They need to feel validated at all times.   Despite all their negative traits, they usually do well and are self-sufficient. They must keep in mind though, that their own arrogance can limit them from growing, and become the cause of their downfall.

Type 3 at a glance

- **Virtue:** Being authentic. When a Type 3 is at peace, they will see no reason to be dishonest or bend to rules. They think themselves to be winners without the need to cheat.
- **Vice:** Deceit and trickery. When not winning, a Type 3 will bend their own moral code to get back on track to victory, despite what they may have to do to get there.
- **Common Temptation:** Being better than others. Bragging and trying too hard is common with Type 3's.
- **Common Desire:** Giving value to whatever enterprise they are involved in.
- **Common Fear:** Not having value. They often worry about being worthless or replaceable.
- **Exalted Ideals:** Hope. Even when down, a Type 3 does not give up easily. Where there is a will, there is a way. They truly believe that the effort they put in will return to them.
- **Egoic Challenge:** Conceit. It can be very difficult for a Type 3 to humble themselves. If another person humbles them, it can be crushing.
- **Integration Point:** 6
- **Disintegration Point:** 9

Type 4: The Individualist and Romantic

Type 4s have a longing desire to be noticed as being one of a kind. They are known as romantics due to their sensitivity. If something in their life lacks meaning, they will find a way to give it meaning. These sorts of people are not afraid to probe themselves and look for deeper significance throughout their days. Many people with a Type 4 personality make great artists and inventors. They do not chase after other people, preferring to give off an air of mystery and have others chase them. When someone does make an effort to know them, they often appreciate the sentiment. They may, however, try to pass their emotions onto others as a tactic to invoke compassion from people.

Type 4s feel a need to express how unique they are. Being individuals and not being lobbed into groups is important to them. When a Type 4 is operating on a higher polarity, they are content, even if they remain sensitive. They are acutely aware of what their emotions are and will probe deeper if need be. Diving into the darker side of the self can take great amounts of courage, and even if it is not always on display, Type 4s are willing to explore sides of themselves that others often avoid. They are also very good at finding the missing pieces and can solve many riddles and puzzles. The creativity of Type 4s knows almost no boundary. These combinations of characteristics can create a person that is very driven and can be an inspiration to others.

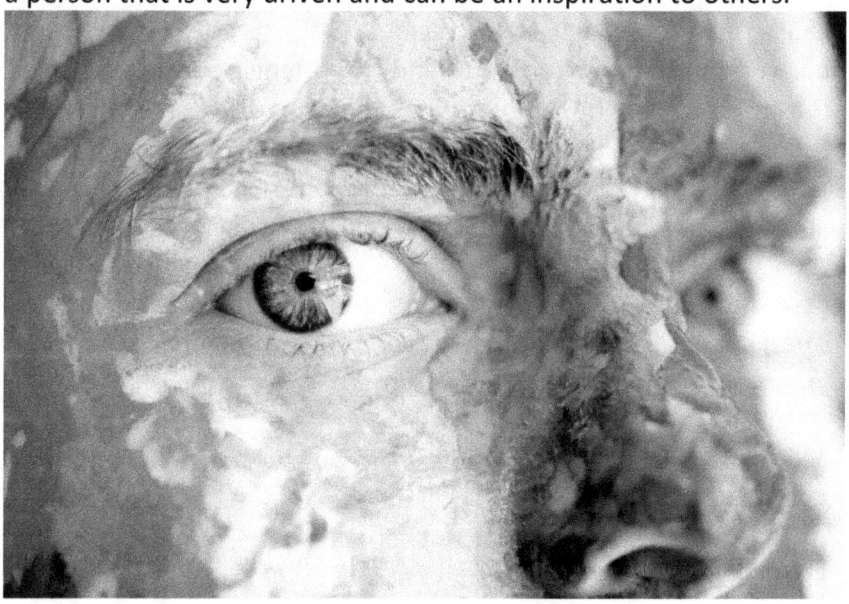

Feelings are always at the front of a Type 4's mind. They can pick up on the subtle hints of themselves, others, and the environment. They may even be able to pick out emotions in people before the other person notices it themselves. Not a single area in the spectrum of emotions is alien to a Type 4. This can have a negative side effect though. They can come across to others as temperamental and can be victims of mood swings. Switching from extreme joy to extreme sadness within minutes can happen to type 4s and keep them out of balance. They tend to take life a bit too seriously and may have trouble lightening up.

They seek out people that they can share the depths of their thought and feelings with. This can create long-lasting bonds, or they may come across as annoying to others. Since a 4 is usually looking for deeper meaning, they do not excel at small talk. They can exaggerate many of their own stories and place the emphasis of most conversations on themselves.

Typically, a 4 will feel that something is missing in their life. This can cause them to easily become envious of other people. They also may harp on the negative too much and beat themselves up for no good reason. They may have a plethora of amazing qualities about themselves but ignore them, and instead focus on what is wrong. They also have trouble separating emotions from other aspects of life and can become very bias, even bigotry. They place more trust in their own experiences and may not take advice or criticism well. A Type 4 needs to go to great lengths to keep up their esteem, and they often get easily bored with mundane routines. All in all, a Type 4 is looking to be understood and accepted.

More often than not, other types of people will feel pushed away by 4s. Their unique natures and need to create deep bonds can repel people away, as Type 4s may not come across as fun or easygoing. Some people may consider them to be downers, always focusing on what is missing in life. They are often labeled as bad listeners, even though they are usually very good at listening. They require more time to express themselves, and this can cause them to get left behind or feel as if they were. They do not like to be interrupted while expressing themselves.

They may want to continue pursuing something after it has already finished, beating a dead horse. Type 4s have also been labeled as drama queens or being melodramatic. Yet, when a Type 4 places all their emotional energy into some form of art, they often can stir the emotions of other people as deeply as their own water of emotion is raging in themselves.

In the end, a Type 4 wants to learn everything they can about themselves. They are self-explorers. This makes them naturals when it comes to spiritual pursuits. They are willing to go both into the dark and the light. They are natural loners but do not want to be. For Type 4s who are aiming for spiritual ascension, they can often find the companionship they are looking for in search of the divine.

Type 4 at a glance

- **Virtue:** Balancing their emotions. When a Type 4 is operating at their best, they can steady the violent waters and maintain peace through emotional adversity and confusion.
- **Vice:** Envy. A Type 4 can easily become jealous of something that another person has since they are always searching for the missing pieces of their life.
- **Common Temptation:** Daydreaming. A Type 4 has to go to great efforts to remain grounded.
- **Common Desire:** To be themselves without any justification or reasoning.
- **Common Fear:** Losing their identity or purpose.
- **Exalted Ideals:** Genesis. A Type 4 can peel back the curtains of mystery and see how a series of events began. They can think backward, which helps when they are trying to understand themselves.
- **Egoic Challenge:** Overindulgence in fantasy. Again, they have to go to great efforts to remain grounded here on earth.
- **Integration Point:** 1
- **Disintegration Point:** 2

Type 5: The Investigator and Observer

These are the quiet types of people. They would rather practice silence to absorb as much information as they can. Type 5s feel a longing to shatter ignorance and understand exactly how the world around them works. Acquisition of knowledge and seeing things in the bigger picture is what they aim to do. They are usually private people and will defend their independence fiercely. They can be frugal and may not share their resources. They can also be visionaries though and are able to root themselves in the present moment. They have an acute ability to maintain focus. They are capable of detaching themselves from circumstance and remain balanced in thought.

Type 5s can also be recognized as being arrogant or too guarded by other people. They may take the defensive more than the offensive and walk around with a shield that prevents others from getting close to them. By striving to do everything on their own, they can sometimes intimidate or offend people without trying to. They may also act as minimalists. They do not need many material possessions, but those that they do have, they cherish very deeply.

They are good problem solvers and can extrapolate complexities down into more manageable forms. Often, a Type 5 is thought of as someone deep and insightful. They also can come up with inventive ideas and find solutions to problems that stymie other people. Their curious and probing nature can seem to lack emotions, and some people may view Type 5s more as robots than humans. Many of them are intellectuals which can either be a blessing or a curse when trying to bond with others.

These are the most natural loners. They do not do it to look cool either. They genuinely like spending time alone and not being hassled by other people's issues. Privacy and security are very important to type them. Don't expect them to rearrange their plans to make someone else feel good. A Type 5 may adopt the mindset of living without a want instead of pursuing it if it takes up too much of their time. If someone wants to get to know a Type 5, then they will have to present something of interest to them. Otherwise, the Type 5 will continue to study whatever they are already engaged in.

Mentally, Type 5s have a natural ability to compartmentalize information. They can separate one thing from another instead of being bogged down by too many overlapping correspondences. This ability helps with their constant gathering of new information. They are also more left-brained, as in they think with the heads instead of their hearts. Emotions are another form of intellect to a Type 5, and they would rather think something through than feel it out. This can explode in the face of a Type 5 when they need an emotional outlet and do not look for one. They can become emotionally drained without realizing it and suffer negative consequences.

A Type 5 needs to let go of control. They know that they cannot control everything but may still try to do so anyway, creating a form of cognitive dissonance. They can also come across as rigid, guarded, and cold to other people. They can seem brutally arrogant and snobbish. They also do not give second chances very often. These traits can make bonding with a Type 5 very taxing, and people will give up on them. In turn, Type 5s give up on others just as easily.

Type 5s can have trouble feeling content since they think there is always more to learn. Even when they are content, they may mask it. They can also be a bit hard to follow and understand since they often refuse to see things from another – lesser – person's point of view. They can be mistaken for being greedy as well. Their loner nature makes establishing relationships very difficult. They can also place too much importance on their mind and ignore other aspects of life such as their reputations.

Spiritually speaking, a type 5 can use their focus and intellect to rise onto higher plains. They are also good at removing distractions and can use that to their advantage by placing spiritual work before everything else. Or, they can get too caught up in their intellect and forget to balance out the other aspects of themselves, thus, preventing them from acceding onto a higher sphere. They can struggle to find the medium between living for themselves and living for others.

Type 5 at a glance

- **Virtue:** Letting go. Type 5s can forget the past and move into the future.
- **Vice:** Grudge. This can act as the opposite of letting go. They can hoard onto the past and get trapped in the present, never being able to step into the future.
- **Common Temptation:** Misinterpretations. The tendency of a Type 5 to think in the bigger picture all the time can prevent them from noticing the importance of smaller details.
- **Common Desire:** To understand everything around them.
- **Common Fear:** Remaining in ignorance.

- **Exalted Ideals:** Human omniscience. They do not know all, but they can connect the dots so well that they may come across almost as psychic.
- **Egoic Challenge:** Not giving. Type 5s have to overcome their loner nature and let other people in, as well as share their wisdom and resources.
- **Integration Point:** 8
- **Disintegration Point:** 7

Type 6: The Loyalist and Skeptic

Type 6s swing on both ends of polarity. They can be the most excessive of worriers or the most trusting of all the dominant personality types. The main drives in their lives revolve around being safe and secure. They want to trust the world around them, but to be on the safe side, they will opt for preparation more than faith. They can share their trust openly or become showered by fear and clam up in a shell. It really can go either way. A Type 6 may walk around all day trying to balance both their trust and skepticism. They often won't let their guard down even though they long to.

Their devotion makes them some of the best team players that anyone will ever meet. Unless a type 6 becomes fearful, they will only bring benefits to whatever team they join. They have a high moral code and will defend other people and do what they can to uphold what they consider to be just. It may not be apparent when first meeting a 6, but they are very courageous. They have to be since fear is always trying to creep up on them. They do not abstain from commitments either. When a 6 makes a pledge, they will see it through. They are often prepared for the rougher patches of life as well. Type 6s are survivors.

Remember though, that there are many different versions of each personality type. A type 6 on the lower polarity can become obsessed with their fears. They are susceptible to phobias and paranoia.

Anxiety can get the best of them. They are prone to bouts of confusion and may lack direction. Or, they may charge directly into their fears and deftly conquer them. Typically, a Type 6 will bounce from one extreme to the other. Some days, they will be too rattled to get much of anything done. On other days, they will be a force of efficiency and victory. Either way, they are very responsible people.

A Type 6 will look into their environment for challenges and solutions. They can become very effective problem solvers if they do not let their fears get the best of them. However, they can also be wary of solving a lot of problems simply by not trusting the solutions they come up with.

6s like to have trust in authority. They look for people of authority in their relationships and hope that those who have authority will help keep them safe. They always keep in mind though that those with authority can betray them, so this creates a wayward relationship often. Type 6s are known to ask a lot of questions of both friends and strangers alike. The more information they have, the more they can prepare themselves to remain safe.

The most important thing for a 6 to do is not focus on their fears. If their fears get out of hand, they can project them onto other people. When focusing on the positive, they are capable of bonding with almost anyone, but doing so is a constant challenge for them. They have to be careful not to drive people away by expressing too much fear. They are very in tune with their emotions and usually can detect the root cause of how they are feeling.

When functioning on a lower polarity, they can come across as a pessimist. Their attention to trust can also have a reverse effect. People may become suspicious of them, and in turn, not trust them. 6s also tend to look too far into the future and worry about things that may never happen.

When a 6 is on a spiritual path, they must remember to maintain balance. Loyalty is a form of faith. Skepticism is a form of fear. Being either on one end or the other can lead them astray. They must find a middle ground and hold onto it if they are to rise to a higher plane of understanding.

Type 6 at a glance

- **Virtue:** Courage. A Type 6 can face their fears and crush them.
- **Vice:** Fear. If they do not face their fears, then they will be in a constant state of questioning everything.
- **Common Temptation:** Not making a choice. A Type 6 may choose inaction and not accomplish much of anything.
- **Common Desire:** To be given a clear roadmap of what to do. They would rather have others make decisions for them.
- **Common Fear:** Not having a roadmap and being left to figure out everything for themselves.
- **Exalted Ideals:** Absolute faith. This can lead them to overcome anything.
- **Egoic Challenge:** They need to focus on the positive instead of the negative.
- **Integration Point:** 9
- **Disintegration Point:** 3

Type 7: The Enthusiast

7s long to get the most that they can out of life. These are optimistic people and like to focus on the positive side of life. They enjoy play and can be thrill seekers. They can be either relaxed and pleasant or impulsive and easily distracted.

They require freedom, so they don't miss out on the opportunities that life can offer them. This makes them rather flexible and adventurous. They often like to look ahead at what tomorrow may bring. They can also become very focused and practical when trying to make sure that the future they envision will become reality.

A 7 can have trouble slowing down their mind. When introduced to a stimulus, they may have trouble ignoring it. This leads to rapid thoughts that may help or hurt them. Limitations do not sit well with 7s. When given the freedom to learn as they go, they excel in whatever they are doing.

7s are strong starters but poor finishers. Many jobs they start will never be finished. They will move onto the next thing before finishing the last. This is because they get bored very easily and need constant stimulation. Some of them can come across as adrenaline junkies and may be too wild for some people's taste. They can also be fidgety and jump from one topic to another before coming to any concrete conclusions. They are not the most patient people and have to be aware go to great lengths to not become restless.

These people are the life of the party and attention seekers. To some, this can come across as a flaw while others will view 7's as a source of raw energy. They can be hyper and have trouble calming down even in formal situations. They can also be escapist, and instead of solving their problems, they will just avoid them. They can also rewrite history in their minds and turn a negative experience into a positive one, which will delay them learning lessons properly. They do not handle well being told what to do or not do and can be prone to fights. However, they also tend to try and use humor to soften any negative vibes.

They tend to avoid facing their fears which can stunt their growth. They do not realize that always having a positive mindset in itself is limiting. They are also poor listeners since their minds are always racing a mile a minute. They tend to avoid looking at themselves and instead, blame other people for other things that have gone wrong.

When a 7 is on a spiritual path, they must remember to calm down. There is a proper time to use all their energy, but it can also lead them to believe in things that simply are not true. If a 7 can learn to direct their energy correctly, then they can open up astral gates that were previously closed. If they don't learn how to control their energy, they will only delude themselves into thinking they have reached a higher plane of being, when in reality, they have only been running in circles.

Type 7 at a glance

- **Virtue:** Sobriety. A typical 7 does not need any substance to make life more interesting for them.
- **Vice:** Overindulgence. When not controlled, their affirming nature can get out of hand and lead to excess.
- **Common Temptation:** Always looking outward for the next thrill. They should look more within to find completion.
- **Common Desire:** To feel fulfilled.
- **Common Fear:** Not having freedom.
- **Exalted Ideals:** Pain and wisdom. If a 7 can focus their energy on both understanding the positive and negative, they can literally accomplish anything.
- **Egoic Challenge:** Always anticipating what comes next. 7s need to practice living in the moment instead of looking for the next dose of excitement.
- **Integration Point:** 5
- **Disintegration Point:** 1

Type 8: The Challenger and Protector

Out of all the personality types, this one needs to let go of the need to control more than any other. Having control makes 8s feel as if they have value. They are not comfortable showing vulnerability. These are very strong people, but even the strong have weaknesses. Type 8s need to come to terms with that.

They look forward to challenges and will deftly defend what they value, people or otherwise. Most 8s are personable because they are so strong, others like to be around them and feel the field of their protection. Or, they can be too forceful and may try to overpower others. They often try to appear larger than life, and by doing so can become intimidating. They can also confuse their own sense of worth by thinking they are the most important people on the planet.

They do not depend on other people and rather try to get others to depend upon them. They can be aggressive and quick to action, even hasty at times. When they make a decision, they stick to it, even if it was the wrong choice. They are fighters, and they want everyone to know and respect it.

They like to be the cause, not the effect and can toss influence onto others. Intense and direct are two words that can sum up a Type 8. A common mistake that 8s make is by labeling other people as strong or weak without taking the entire human into consideration. Again, they can be hasty and do not like to admit when they are wrong. They can also view the world either as black or white and are not the best at blending different elements together.

An easy way to offend an 8 is to ignore them. They are larger than life, and by ignoring them, a knife is stabbed into their pride. Another thing that bothers them is giving them a task to do that is beneath them. When 8's are not in charge, they are more likely to rebel then protect. They are also not the best at exploring their emotions. Many human emotions reveal weakness, and 8s are weak to weakness. They may not realize this, but by not admitting their flaws, they are only highlighting those same flaws. They can also easily ruin a good situation by not compromising. Not compromising is also a weakness. They like to make up their own rules and can become rebellious for no good reason. They may also step forward to be a leader when they are not the best suited for the job. When an 8 is in control and everyone is subservient to them, there is no trouble. When they lose control, they can be hellish. Yet, 8s will defend those they care for to the death. They will fight until the battle is won.

Spiritually, an 8 can be comparable to the zodiac sign of Leo. They are a fiery lion, fixed fire. If they can direct their power, and let go of the need for power, they can ascend as high as they want. If they can't control their power and let go, they will keep on fighting the same fight against themselves until the day they die. Another word that should be attributed to the 8s is *passion*. The 8s will either be enslaved by their passions and fall victim to them, or they will win the fight against their passions and use that energy to better themselves. If an 8 can control their passions, then they cannot just reach a higher plane of being but storm the gates of heaven with the raw power of a flaming red lion.

Type 8 at a glance

> **Virtue:** Innocence. Aside from their characteristics, 8's really does not understand that they have flaws. They also don't grasp that they have anything to improve upon. However, if they have put in the work to improve themselves instead of ignoring their negative traits, then they truly are innocent. Innocent – as in free from error.
> **Vice:** Lust. This is not just sexual, but they can be overly forceful.
> **Common Temptation:** Believing they have no limits. At some point, this mindset will destroy them. They have to control their passions.
> **Common Desire:** Not needing anyone else besides themselves.
> **Common Fear:** Being defeated, bested, losing, not being able to protect themselves or others.
> **Exalted Ideals:** Truth. Since they believe in themselves so much, they don't have any reason to purposefully lie, although they lie to themselves often without realizing it.
> **Egoic Challenge:** Vengeance. Again, 8s need to learn to let go and stop the fight.
> **Integration Point:** 2
> **Disintegration Point:** 5

Type 9: The Peacemaker and Mediator

People of this type are in a constant search for harmony, not just for themselves but also for the rest of the world. Peace, stability, and balance are few words used to describe Type 9s. Type 9s will go far out of their way to avoid conflict. These people would rather choose to avoid arguments even if doing so besmirches their reputations. On a lower polarity, they may act as procrastinators.

When viewing the word *mediator* of the Type 9 personality, don't think of it so much as a negotiation between two people, but linking the peace of nature with themselves. Such a statement may sound abstract, but Type 9s are cut from a different cloth. They seek to be at one with the world and universe.

The emotions and actions of other people can greatly affect Type 9s. They do not have a high tolerance against others who are in bad moods and will often try to lift their spirits, or just ignore them. They are fantastic listeners and are able to see any situation from several different points of view. They are patient and very supportive of other people.

9s have an innate ability to let go and move on. Because of this, they seem to have a great impact on the environment around them. 9s often choose not to disturb the peace around them which can present them as pacifists to other people. They can also be a predictable group and often choose daily patterns that help keep them at ease. They live to avoid conflict and stress.

9s would rather form tight bonds with people than have a superficial relationship. They often feel very intense emotions but are capable of maintaining them and remaining even-tempered. This can mask the truth of how a 9 is really feeling as they may choose to not project their true feelings onto others, leaving people wondering what they are really thinking.

9s can be stubborn. They may be so averse to conflict that they simply let unjust actions happen without doing anything to stop them. In their pursuit of being in harmony with everyone, they can keep too much of an open mind at times and may let wickedness go unchallenged. They can show the darker side of mercy, as in being merciful to those who are wicked and by proxy, spreading more wickedness. They may also try to remain calm when they are really not, and by doing so, they wind up masking their true selves which will keep them out of balance with those they are trying to bond with. They cannot also recognize some of their more negative aspects and take a very long time to improve their weaknesses.

They do not manage anger well. Being angry to a 9 can sap all of their energy, and then they will suffer a long spell of lethargy. It can take them a very long time to recover from an argument or bout of anger. In fact, they may not even notice that they are upset and avoid the conflict going on within themselves. This causes them to not develop the proper coping skills to deal with anger, and they never get any better at managing it. This is one of their biggest challenges to remaining at peace.

The ironic thing about a 9 is that they are not easy to manipulate. Since they can let go so easily, they can just walk away. This can confound the people that are trying to influence them. By letting go, the 9 has gained more control. A 9 may also, when they finally do express their opinion, be long-winded in their explanations. This can make them a bore to many other people and difficult to communicate with.

9s often display passive aggressive behavior without realizing it. This can be a damaging blow to their reputations. Type 9s are often the targets of gossip but will not do anything to stop it. They will simply accept it and carry on.

Spiritually, Type 9s are proponents of meditation. They are the calm waters. The only major downside to this is leaving wickedness unchecked. A type 9 may be able to raise their consciousness, but when they re-enter the world of other people, they will have a hard time maintaining their peace. So, they will walk away again, let go, and repeat the pattern all over. If anything, they need to be a bit more assertive and not shy away from conflict. If a type 9 were to seek their highest virtues, which involve proper discernment of consequences for their actions, they very well may be able to ascend past the normal boundary of human perception. Of course, such a platitude would take much training, but they aim to be at total peace with nature and accomplishing such a feat will not come quickly no matter what techniques they use.

9 is a number of completions, the last digit before a new cycle begins again. If someone with the dominant personality of a 9 were to put in the work and understand that there may come a time when they will have to end their passivity and step into action, then a whole new world of wisdom may just be found resting at their feet. If they find that new wisdom and understand it, then they can reenter the world of other people and be able to maintain their sense of peace better than before.

Type 9 at a glance

- **Virtue:** Action orientated. This does not mean that Type 9s jump into action, but that they are able to discern between which actions will have bad consequences. This is a major reason why they often choose to not act and maintain passive.
- **Vice:** Laziness. When a 9 is not operating at their best, they may take inaction too far and not do much of anything.
- **Common Temptation:** To avoid stress, conflict, and not take chances or stir the pot.
- **Common Desire:** To have peace of mind – no more problems.
- **Common Fear:** Being out of balance with themselves.
- **Exalted Ideals:** Love. Don't think of love in terms of romance, but more so as the two things being attracted and joined together. They seek the love of nature.
- **Egoic Challenge:** 9s have to try hard to remain down to earth and remember that life is a balance between the positive and the negative. They must keep in mind that one cannot exist without the other.
- **Integration Point:** 3
- **Disintegration Point:** 6

Chapter 5: The Wings

The Wings are the secondary personality traits. These are the less apparent pieces of the human psyche that mix in with the dominant personality. Your secondary personality traits can not only add to the pool of the self, but it can sometimes be in direct opposition to a dominant personality. This concept is often overlooked.

To fully understand the self, every aspect (no matter how small) of the personality must be observed. Take a look at the image of the Enneagram again. As you know, there are 9 dominant types of personalities. To explain the Wings, we will use number 9 (The Peacemaker and Mediator) as an example. 9 is between 1, and 8. 1 and 8 are the Wings of someone who has a Type 9 personality.

Yes, it's that simple. Whatever your dominant personality number is, the numbers to its right and left are its wings. Someone who is a 9 will have all of the characteristics of either a 1 or an 8, a perfectionist or a challenger. These will always be secondary to the dominant personality traits, but they are still always active at the same time. So not only do you have to learn everything you can about your dominant personality to truly know yourself, but you must also learn the proponents of your Wing as well. Maybe it is not so simple. Self-discovery is a lifelong process, and the journey will not end until the life does.

Some people only have one wing, while others have two. Figuring out what your Wing is can be very tricky, and if you are unsure whether you have one or two, then the road to illumination can become even more confusing. The best advice that can be given to assist with this is to figure out what your dominant personality is, and then look at both of the possible Wings. If one of the descriptions for a Wing resonates with you more than another, begin focusing on that. If both of the Wings resonate, select one to focus on first and learn as much about it as you can before moving onto the next one. Don't attempt to discover or alter too much about yourself all at once. There may be a temptation to do so, but it is better to work slowly with the Enneagram in the beginning.

It should be made clear that just knowing your dominant personality type and its Wing will not give you the full spectrum of the personality. There are also the integration/disintegration points and different levels of health-related to how someone's personality expresses itself. Due to so many different factors being involved, two separate people who are both Type 3 (or any other number) may behave quite differently. To fully understand your own personality, remember this formula. Write it down next to the diagram of the Enneagram you were told to draw earlier in this book.

Dominant Personality + Wing(s) + Integration point + Disintegration point + Health Level of Personality = TRUE SELF
To clarify, let's use personality type 3 as an example. 3 is between the numbers 2 and 4. For this example, we will assume that 2 is the Wing. We will also assume that the current level of health for this example is a 5. We know that the integration point for a 3 is 6 and the disintegration point is 9.

Dominant Personality **(3)** + Wing(s) **(2)** + Integration point **(3)** + Disintegration point **(6)** + Health Level of Personality **(5)** = TRUE SELF **(3, 2, 3, 6, 5)**

Many people have wrongly tried to promote the Enneagram as a fast track to self-discovery. This is not how the Enneagram was meant to be used. The Enneagram is meant to be studied and meditated upon time and time again. The Enneagram is meant to be fully understood that someone can use it to summon up different personas and become the type of person they need to be for whatever challenge they have to face.

Think of it like this; you live inside the Enneagram as your dominant personality with both its positive and negative traits. As you move through life inside the Enneagram, you learn how to shed your dominant personality when coming across a challenge that it cannot overcome and adopt one of the other personality types to defeat the challenge your dominant personality lacked the tools to deal with. Later, you will always return to your dominant personality as that is your main house. To do this would make you a master of the Enneagram, and thus, a master of life.

Chapter 6: Health of the Self

When two different people both have the same dominant personality type, they may still behave quite differently. This is not just because of the Wings, but also the level of health (or development) that someone's personality is currently at. If two Type 1s are at different levels of health, then the characteristics of their dominant personality will not manifest exactly the same. Someone who is healthier than someone else of the same type or at a higher stage of development will be able to control their negative traits easier.

For example, one of the negative traits of a Type 8 is that they can be domineering and intimidating. If a Type 8 is currently at an average stage of health, then they will probably fluctuate back and forth between controlling their domineering nature and being controlled by it. If they are healthier, above the average range, then they will be able to control their domineering nature better and only use it when needed. If they are lower than the average range, they will have no control and will constantly be projecting their forcefulness on everyone around them. However, a positive aspect of a Type 8 is that they can protect what they care about. If they are in the average range of health, then they will be able to correctly pick and choose who and what they want to protect. If they are above the average range of health, then they will not only be able to protect what they care about but be able to use the right amount of force – and select the correct strategy – when playing the role of a defender. If they are below the average range of health, then they won't so much protect something but simply become a rebel without a cause and argue just to argue without protecting anything in the process.

This is an extremely important part of studying the Enneagram because it is one of the explanations for why and how someone's personality can change with time. None of the levels of heath are locked in place. During one single day, someone may move about the scale of health rapidly depending on the amounts of stress and good luck they are encountering. To truly know yourself though, you still have to pinpoint where your personalities' current level of health is.

There are 9 different levels of health which are all grouped into three separate sets. We will start at the bottom, the unhealthiest level, and work our way to the top.

Unhealthy Levels

Level 9: Self-Destruction – At this stage, the person does not have any control over their personality. They are nothing more than a walking ego that reacts to the world around them. They are like a deer that runs away when scared or a dog that bites the hand that feeds it out of impulse or confusion. They don't think, only act. They don't build themselves up, only destroy. They have absolutely no control over themselves. Spiritually speaking, this is the stage of Hell.

Level 8: Obsessive Compulsion – At this level, someone does maintain some control over their actions, but only to a small degree. Subconscious habits dictate the person's patterns and activities. There is often a cycle of repetition at this stage. The body will do several small tasks without the self-conscious realizing it. These behaviors may not be self-destructive but can fall into that category if not managed properly.

Level 7: Violation – This is when the person is beginning to cause harm to themselves. They have awareness that they lack self-control but can't do much to counteract it. They are violating their own will. They know something is wrong and want improvement but continue to defy themselves. Many people with addictions they want to quit are operating at this level. In other areas of their lives, they may actually have self-control, but every time they give into the addiction again, they drop down to this level, if only for a short time.

Average Levels

Level 6: Overcompensation – One level below self-control. The mind will recognize that there is a lack of willpower, and instead of working directly on the trouble areas, the subconscious will exaggerate the qualities that the self-conscious does have control over. Compare it to the basketball player that can't shoot a free-throw but can perform a slam dunk. Instead of improving their free-throw, they will constantly go for more slam dunks.

Level 5: Self-Control – This is the medium level that most people operate on. When you wake up in the morning, you are probably working at this stage. There is self-control, but it can be altered depending on what else happens through the course of the day.

Level 4: Social Control – People at this stage can maintain their self-control even when the environment around them is trying to influence them. They are not swayed, for better or worse, by peer pressure or social conventions. They remain true to themselves even while the world is fluctuating around them.

Healthy Levels

Level 3: Social Understanding – This is when someone truly knows their place and value in the world. They fully grasp the effect they have on others as well as the effect others have on them. People at this stage are not swayed by stimulus or moral conventions. No matter what is going on or where they are, they remain in control of themselves.

Level 2: Psychological Understanding – Many would describe this stage as the highest point a person can reach. This is a true and complete understanding of who you are. You recognize your vices, virtues, and can alter both of them at any given time no matter where you are or what is going on. Even when someone changes their personality to a different level, people who have been at this stage can recognize the change and manage things properly. When people reach the second level, they can control their desires, alter their personality as they need to, and move about the Enneagram as they want. They can trace every thought and emotion back to its source and stop those emotions from escalating.

Level 1: Self Freedom – Most people never reach or can even fathom this stage. This is the level of absolute control. The personality can be completely altered by the person at their command. All impulses and urges are switches that the person can turn on or off as they see fit. There are no desires or questions. The person is at total peace with who they are. Spiritually speaking, this is complete unity with God. According to some authorities on the Enneagram, this stage is beyond human comprehension.

Integration and Disintegration Points

The above-mentioned levels of health are in regard to how the entire personality changes as a whole. The integration and disintegration points only relate to how the dominant personality changes.

When a stressful stimulus interacts with someone, the stress will cause their personality to drop or disintegrate into another type of personality. Opposite of that, when someone receives good fortune, their personality will grow or integrate into another type of personality. When feeling good or bad, a different dominant personality type will take over temporarily. If someone has a Type 1 dominant personality functioning at a level 6 of health, and they become stressed, they will behave like a Type 4 functioning at a level 6 of health. If that same person, a Type 1 functioning at a level 6 of health, receives good fortune, then they will behave like a Type 7 functioning at a level 6 of health. They will always return to their dominant personality type afterward, and the integration/disintegration points do not affect the overall level of health that they are currently functioning on.

The mind needs a way to deal with stress and luck. Temporarily moving from one personality type to another, but always having a dominant type to return to, is nature's way of letting people segment different aspects of themselves. This is why it is important to remember that there is no superior personality. The levels of health are the only piece of the personality that can be considered superior or inferior. With proper knowledge about the self and effort, the levels of health can be altered since none of them are set in stone. The integration/disintegration points are just another part of who you really are.

Integration Points

When someone receives a boost to their mood, they will temporarily switch from their normal dominant personality to another dominant personality. The flow of integration is as follows;

- A Type 1 will behave as a Type 7.
- A Type 2 will behave as a Type 4.
- A Type 3 will behave as a Type 6.
- A Type 4 will behave as a Type 1.
- A Type 5 will behave as a Type 8.
- A Type 6 will behave as a Type 9.
- A Type 7 will behave as a Type 1.
- A Type 8 will behave as a Type 2.
- A Type 9 will behave as a Type 3.

Disintegration Points

When someone becomes stressed, they will temporarily switch from their normal dominant personality to another dominant personality. The flow of disintegration is as follows;

- A Type 1 will behave as a Type 4.
- A Type 2 will behave as a Type 8.
- A Type 3 will behave as a Type 9.
- A Type 4 will behave as a Type 2.
- A Type 5 will behave as a Type 7.
- A Type 6 will behave as a Type 3.
- A Type 7 will behave as a Type 1.
- A Type 8 will behave as a Type 5.
- A Type 9 will behave as a Type 6.

Now that you have been fully introduced to the Enneagram, this formula is worth repeating.

Dominant Personality + Wing(s) + Integration point + Disintegration point + Health Level of Personality = TRUE SELF

Chapter 7: Personality Test

Please bear in mind that general personality tests may not resonate with everyone or be entirely accurate. If you expect a quick test to tell you everything about who you really are, you have been misled by charlatans and fads. Consider this personality test a start to self-discovery and only a start, nothing more. This should give you a basic starting point to figure out your dominant personality type. For the level of health regarding your personality, you will have to determine that yourself (but remember that it can fluctuate). For the integration/disintegration points, check the earlier references listed in this book.

Get a pen and piece of paper. Write down your answers to these questions. Every time you answer YES, write down the number 1 for your answer. Every time you answer NO, write down the number 2. Every time you answer SOMEWHAT, write down the number 3. Every time you answer UNSURE, write down the number 4. Different parts of the test are allotted to different types of dominant personality types. At the end, you will tally up your score for each section. There are 10 questions to each part. The minimal score for each part is 10. The maximum is 40. What is most important about this test is not the overall score. What you need to pay attention to is what area you have scored lowest or highest in.

PART 1

I begin planning my next project before the current one is completed.
YES   NO   SOMEWHAT   UNSURE

I have everything I want in my life.
YES   NO   SOMEWHAT   UNSURE

I would rather stay at home on my day off than go out.

YES   NO   SOMEWHAT   UNSURE

I like to stay awake all night.
YES   NO   SOMEWHAT   UNSURE

I am a morning person.
YES   NO   SOMEWHAT   UNSURE

I think there is life after death.
YES   NO   SOMEWHAT   UNSURE

New people frighten me.
YES NO   SOMEWHAT   UNSURE

I only like to be with other people who share my interests.
YES   NO   SOMEWHAT   UNSURE

I think therapy is for the weak.
YES   NO   SOMEWHAT   UNSURE

I would rather work alone than with other people.
YES   NO   SOMEWHAT   UNSURE

PART 2

I do not like receiving negative feedback.
YES   NO   SOMEWHAT   UNSURE

The world is unfair.
YES   NO   SOMEWHAT   UNSURE

I am very critical towards both myself and others.
YES   NO   SOMEWHAT   UNSURE

I want to be recognized as being successful.
YES   NO   SOMEWHAT   UNSURE

I never become depressed.
YES   NO   SOMEWHAT   UNSURE

I give strangers the benefit of the doubt.
YES   NO   SOMEWHAT   UNSURE

I want people to trust me.
YES   NO   SOMEWHAT   UNSURE

I try to get people with authority to consider me as an equal.
YES   NO   SOMEWHAT   UNSURE

When stressed, I do not make decisions.
YES   NO   SOMEWHAT   UNSURE

I enjoy helping others.
YES   NO   SOMEWHAT   UNSURE

PART 3

People admire me, and I like it.
YES   NO   SOMEWHAT   UNSURE

I can easily calm my emotions.
YES   NO   SOMEWHAT   UNSURE

I do not like expressing my emotions to other people.
YES   NO   SOMEWHAT   UNSURE

When bothered by negativity, I can distract myself with other activities.
YES   NO   SOMEWHAT   UNSURE

I lack ambition.
YES   NO   SOMEWHAT   UNSURE

I easily recognize errors.
YES   NO   SOMEWHAT   UNSURE

I take more then I give.
YES   NO   SOMEWHAT   UNSURE

I am suspicious even towards people I know well.
YES   NO   SOMEWHAT   UNSURE

I am dominant over other people.
YES   NO   SOMEWHAT   UNSURE

I don't care about other people's problems.
YES   NO   SOMEWHAT   UNSURE

PART 4

I am very organized.
YES   NO   SOMEWHAT   UNSURE

Romance is very important to me.
YES   NO   SOMEWHAT   UNSURE

I do not judge other people.
YES   NO   SOMEWHAT   UNSURE

I often compare myself to others.
YES   NO   SOMEWHAT   UNSURE

Close relationship matters more to me than anything else.
YES   NO   SOMEWHAT   UNSURE

I often wonder if I am the center of gossip.
YES   NO   SOMEWHAT   UNSURE

I am a risk taker.
YES   NO   SOMEWHAT   UNSURE

I am intimidating to others.
YES   NO   SOMEWHAT   UNSURE

I am genuine with other people.
YES   NO   SOMEWHAT   UNSURE

I detest slackers.
YES   NO   SOMEWHAT   UNSURE

PART 5

I hate being interrupted.
YES   NO   SOMEWHAT   UNSURE

I avoid making commitments.
YES   NO   SOMEWHAT   UNSURE

I readily impress people.
YES   NO   SOMEWHAT   UNSURE

I do what others want without resistance.
YES   NO   SOMEWHAT.   UNSURE

I place safety first at all times.
YES   NO   SOMEWHAT   UNSURE

Mood swings are common to me.
YES   NO   SOMEWHAT   UNSURE

I like to explore intense emotions.
YES   NO   SOMEWHAT   UNSURE

I long to fit in with a group.
YES   NO   SOMEWHAT   UNSURE

I am very detail-orientated.
YES   NO   SOMEWHAT   UNSURE

My decisions are based on how much fun I think I will have.
YES   NO   SOMEWHAT   UNSURE

PART 6

I am a loner, but do not want to be.
YES   NO   SOMEWHAT   UNSURE

      I would rather be alone than around other people.
YES   NO   SOMEWHAT   UNSURE

I will help others before I help myself.
YES   NO   SOMEWHAT   UNSURE

I do not handle confrontation well.
YES   NO   SOMEWHAT   UNSURE

I thrive during competition.
YES   NO   SOMEWHAT   UNSURE

I am congenial towards everyone I meet.
YES   NO   SOMEWHAT   UNSURE

      Being considered a failure is my greatest fear.
YES   NO   SOMEWHAT   UNSURE

I am selfish and proud of it.
YES   NO   SOMEWHAT   UNSURE

I have trouble saving money.
YES   NO   SOMEWHAT   UNSURE

      I think that a fight can bring people closer together.
YES   NO   SOMEWHAT   UNSURE

PART 7

I believe there is a good quality to being sad.
YES   NO   SOMEWHAT   UNSURE

I have lots of energy.
YES   NO   SOMEWHAT   UNSURE

I can control my temper.
YES   NO   SOMEWHAT   UNSURE

I never back down from a challenge.
YES   NO   SOMEWHAT   UNSURE

I am slow to start new things.
YES   NO   SOMEWHAT   UNSURE

I will continue to work until the job is done.
YES   NO   SOMEWHAT   UNSURE

I always see the silver lining.
YES   NO   SOMEWHAT   UNSURE

I look for things that are wrong more than things that are right.
YES   NO   SOMEWHAT   UNSURE

Having a spotlight on me makes me anxious.
YES   NO   SOMEWHAT   UNSURE

I lack confidence.
YES   NO   SOMEWHAT   UNSURE

PART 8

I look for the good in people instead of the bad.
YES   NO   SOMEWHAT   UNSURE

I avoid change at all cost.
YES   NO   SOMEWHAT   UNSURE

I am more unique than most people.
YES   NO   SOMEWHAT   UNSURE

I don't ever need help.
YES   NO   SOMEWHAT   UNSURE

I am tough as nails.
YES   NO   SOMEWHAT   UNSURE

Other people are left wondering what I am really thinking.
YES   NO   SOMEWHAT   UNSURE

I am too modest.
YES   NO   SOMEWHAT   UNSURE

I have trouble keeping focus.
YES   NO   SOMEWHAT   UNSURE

I am very disciplined.
YES   NO   SOMEWHAT   UNSURE
I can be dramatic.
YES   NO   SOMEWHAT   UNSURE

PART 9

I second guess myself.
YES   NO   SOMEWHAT   UNSURE

I enjoy fantasy more than reality.
YES   NO   SOMEWHAT   UNSURE

I do not make decisions quickly.
YES   NO   SOMEWHAT   UNSURE

I become bored easily.
YES   NO   SOMEWHAT   UNSURE

I think most people are liars.
YES   NO   SOMEWHAT   UNSURE

I often genuflect.
YES   NO   SOMEWHAT   UNSURE

I fall asleep easily.
YES   NO   SOMEWHAT   UNSURE

I am the life of the party.
YES   NO   SOMEWHAT.   UNSURE

I think of the past often.
YES   NO   SOMEWHAT   UNSURE

I have a vivid imagination.
YES   NO   SOMEWHAT   UNSURE

PART 10

There is always something to be thankful for.
YES   NO   SOMEWHAT   UNSURE

I give people second chances.
YES   NO   SOMEWHAT   UNSURE

If I die tomorrow, I would have no regrets.
YES   NO   SOMEWHAT   UNSURE

When one chapter ends, another will always begin.
YES   NO   SOMEWHAT   UNSURE

I think I am smarter than most people.
YES   NO   SOMEWHAT   UNSURE

I enjoy the great outdoors.
YES   NO   SOMEWHAT   UNSURE

I am careful about what I eat.
YES   NO   SOMEWHAT   UNSURE

I would rather spend time with family more than anyone else.
YES   NO   SOMEWHAT.   UNSURE

I do not like my family.
YES   NO   SOMEWHAT   UNSURE

I often have high expectations.
YES   NO   SOMEWHAT   UNSURE

ANSWER KEY

If you scored highest in parts 1 or 2, you are probably a Type 1.

If you scored highest in parts 2 Or 3, you are probably a Type 2.

If you scored highest in parts 3 or 4, you are probably a Type 3.

If you scored highest in parts 4 or 5, you are probably a Type 4.

If you scored highest in parts 5 or 6, you are probably a Type 5.

If you scored highest in parts 6 or 7, you are probably a Type 6.

If you scored highest in parts 7 or 8, you are probably a Type 7.

If you scored highest in parts 8 or 9, you are probably a Type 8.

If you scored highest in parts 9 or 10, you are probably a Type 9.

These groupings may require some explanation. Let's say you scored highest in section 2. That means you are either a Type 2 or Type 3. Or, if you scored highest in section 4, you are either a Type 3 or 4. A Wing of Type 2 is 3, and a Wing of Type 3 is 2. The other Wing of Type 3 is 4. The Wings of 4 are 3 and 5. This pattern continues throughout the rest of the answer key. This test was designed to take the Wings into account, without being able to directly interact with the test taker (you). That is why the word "either" is listed in the Answer Key. If you scored highest in sections 2, then you can determine that you are probably a Type 2 with a Wing of 3. If you scored highest in section 4, then you can determine that you are probably a Type 4 with a wing of 3. If you scored highest in section 10, then you are probably a Type 9 with a Wing of 1. Yet you could be a Type 9 with a wing of 8. This test may not be entirely conclusive, but again, none really are no matter what anyone tries to tell you. It is a starting point though to lead you in the direction you need to go so you can begin to pinpoint your dominant personality type and wing and get to work discovering the rest of yourself after.

Determining exactly if you have the qualities of both Wings, or only one, can't be entirely concluded with just a simple test. You will have to review the chapter on the 9 different personality types again and look into which Type you believe to be your wing, or if you have more than one Wing.

If you have scored highest in more than one section of the test, then you may want to look at those sections again. Take more time to look over the questions and see if you answered them as truthful as possible. This is a common problem with general personality tests. When many people first try taking one, they often realize they don't know themselves well enough to give honest answers. No one is claiming that you have lied on purpose, but you may have made a mistake out of confusion – or some of these questions you may never have spent much time thinking about.

There are other personality tests out there in the world besides this one. The best thing you can do is take more than just one and see what your average is. If several tests, this one included, determine that you are a Type 6 (just as an example), then you can assume you are a Type 6 and continue your journey from there.

Practical Advice

Taking more than one tests is a good start. Simply putting in the effort to read this book was also a good start. Yet, the only way to really discover who you are is to take a chance and try out new things that you have not done before. Go and meet new people that you usually wouldn't interact with. Go visit a location that is outside of your normal haunts. Take up an activity that you have never done before. Expand your horizons, try new things, soak in new stimulus, and see how you react to them. If you meditate, start exercising, or try a different method of meditation than you have before. If you exercise, start meditating or try out a new form of exercise. If you watch TV, read a book instead. If you are an avid reader, watch some TV. The point is, do something new. If you don't ever try out new things, you will not be able to put your personality to the real test which is called LIFE and see the real practical results firsthand.

Oscar Ichazo seems to have faded away from the spotlight. Although he was the man that helped to reveal the Enneagram, his methods and instructions have fallen by the wayside. It is said that he created dance routines for his students and structured individual tasks and lessons for them to complete to discover their true personality. As Oscar Ichazo has stepped away from the spotlight, so have his techniques. They have been replaced by people who talk more than they do and make false guarantees. It has also been reported that Oscar Ichazo did not support what many people who came after he tried to do with the Enneagram – turn it into a scheme to make money by guaranteeing that self-discovery is right around the corner. Self-improvement takes work and exactly what kind of work is needed will be different on a case by case basis. The absolute best practical advice that can be given will not be found inside this book or any book. It can only be found inside of yourself. That is what the Enneagram was really constructed for in the first place – to give you a starting point for learning more about yourself. A starting point, not the final conclusion. Use the Enneagram to give you a peek behind the curtain that you have hidden from your true-self. After you have gotten a glimpse of who you really are, then you can slowly continue to pull out more and more of your own personal truth until the false personality accepts letting go and hands over the reins of truth to who you really are. If you can accomplish that, then the only thing left to do will be to walk the road of liberation.

Best of luck.

Conclusion

Thank you for making it through to the end of *Enneagram*. Let's hope it was informative and able to provide you with all of the tools you need to achieve your goals whatever they may be.

The next step is to figure out what your dominant personality type is. Then you will have to determine what your Wing is. Make sure you take note of the integration and disintegration points for your dominant personality type. Then you can begin to figure out what level of health your personality is currently at. When you have discovered all of these integral pieces of the personality, you can start to bring them together to discover who you truly are. That is only the beginning of the journey of self-discovery though. If you truly want to know yourself down to the tiniest detail, then you must continue self-examination as you continue to grow older. Remember that the Enneagram is meant to be studied for an entire lifetime. It is an emblem and system of knowledge that will continue to emit enlightenment for as long as someone continues studying it. As you continue to change, the Enneagram will always be there to explain why you have changed, and what you have changed into. Be sure to continue using the Enneagram. Return to it whenever you are bogged down by confusion. It is a tool meant to become a master of yourself.

www.ingramcontent.com/pod-product-compliance
Lightning Source LLC
Chambersburg PA
CBHW071352080526
44587CB00017B/3071